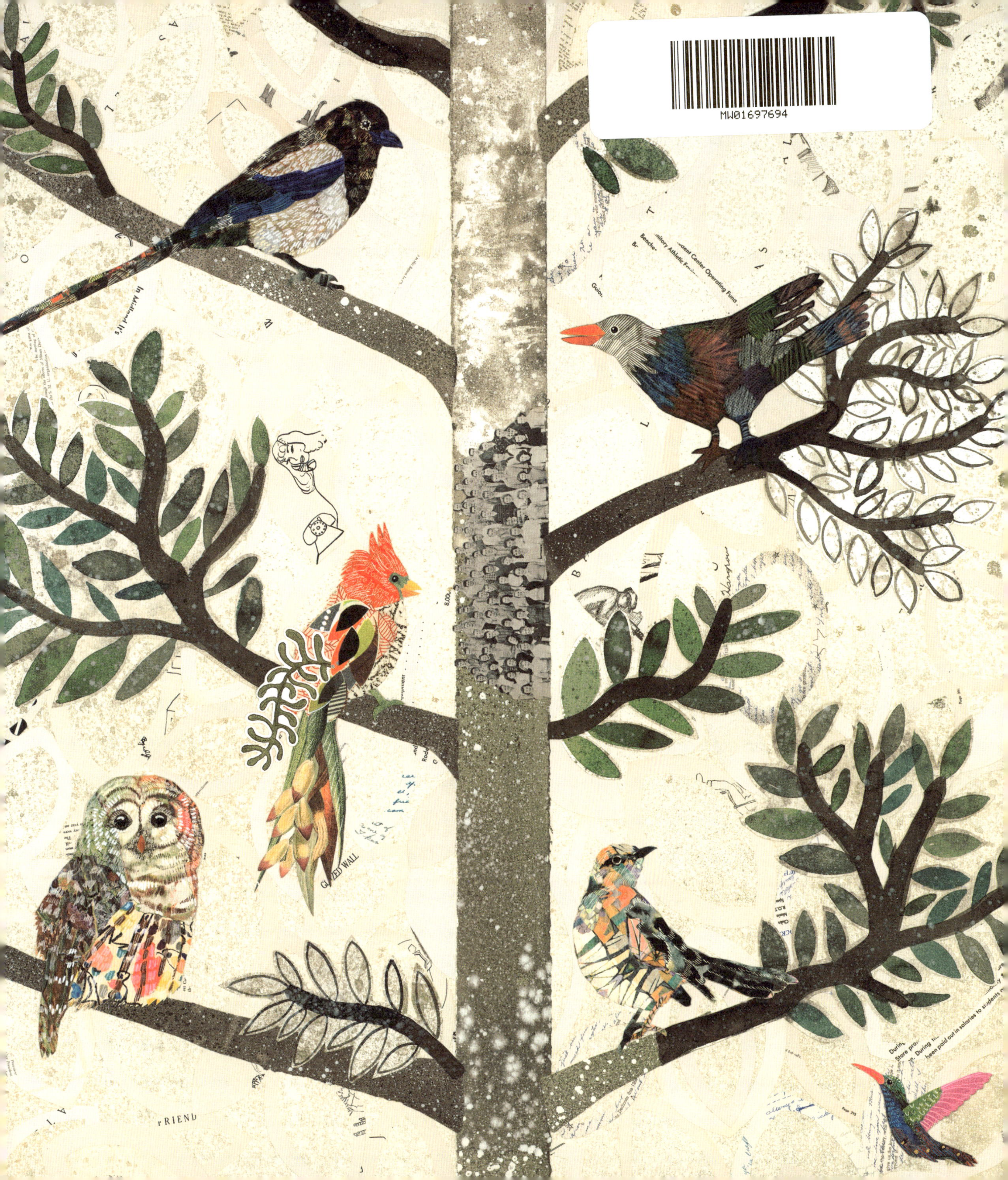

What to Give Up for Lent That's Not Chocolate

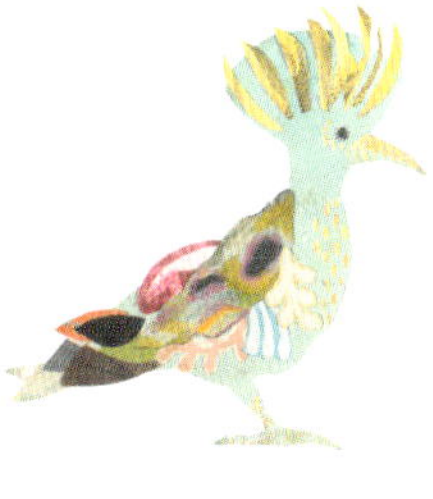

BRENDA BOGART

Published by Cut & Paste Publishing
www.BrendaBogart.com

Half of the net proceeds up to $100,000 will be donated to Feeding America. Please visit www.FeedingAmerica.org.

Printed in the United States

FLUENCY
TELLING STORIES THAT MATTER

Produced with the assistance of Fluency Organization, Inc.

Design by Inkwell Creative

To my husband, Bill
The only person in my life who thinks I'm low maintenance

Bill, you were the first person in my life who
encouraged me to pursue my dreams,
to be who I am in the Lord,
without any expectation of success in the world's eyes,
but simply because God gave me a desire to make art.
I am dedicating this book to you because I fiercely love you
and know with all my heart that I would not be an artist today
without your encouragement.

You are my beloved husband,
my brother in Christ,
and my primary earthly concern.
Love,
Brenda

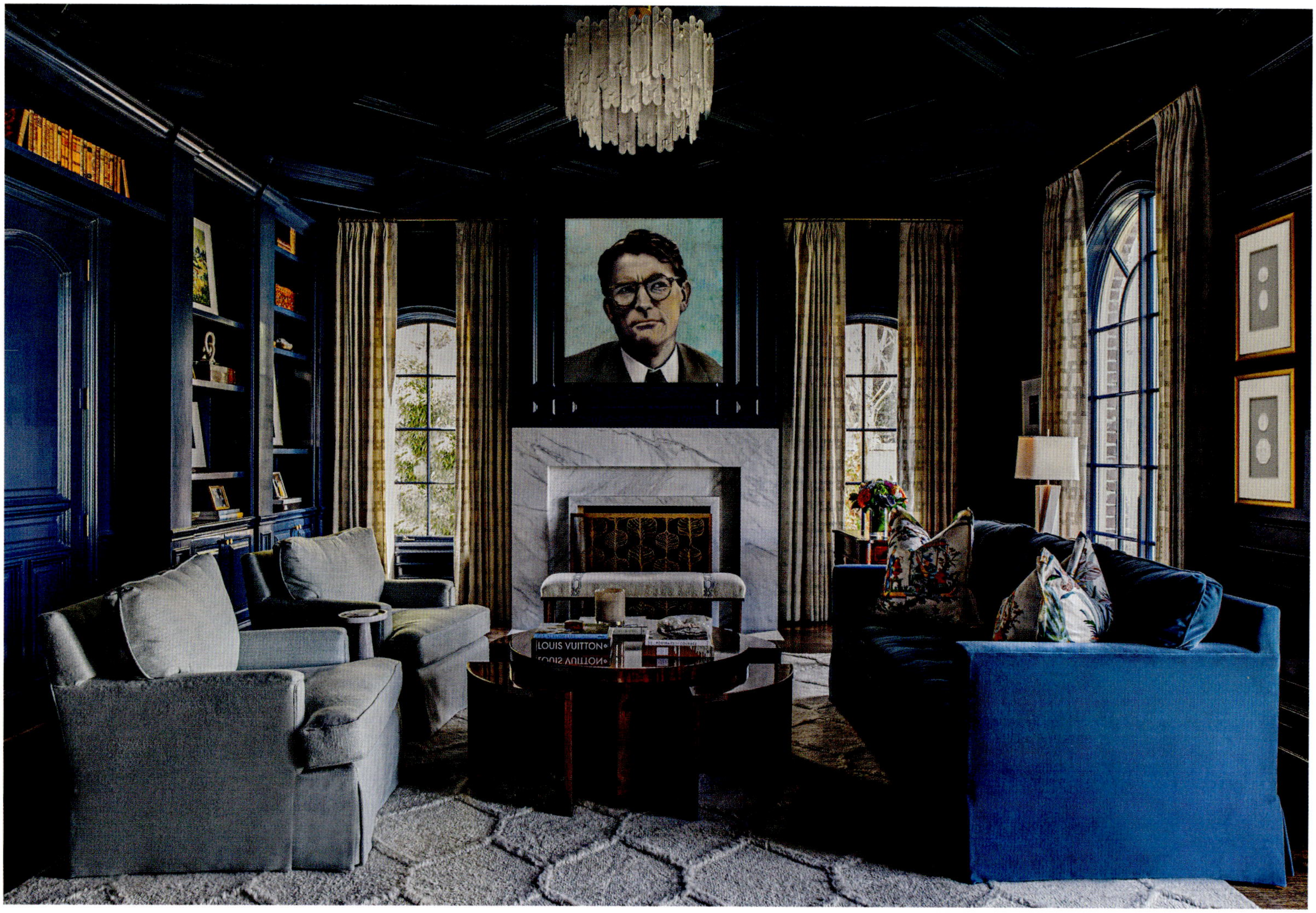

© EMERY DAVIS PHOTOGRAPHY (AMY'S INTERIORS, DALLAS TX; ART THROUGH BLUE PRINT GALLERY)

TABLE OF CONTENTS

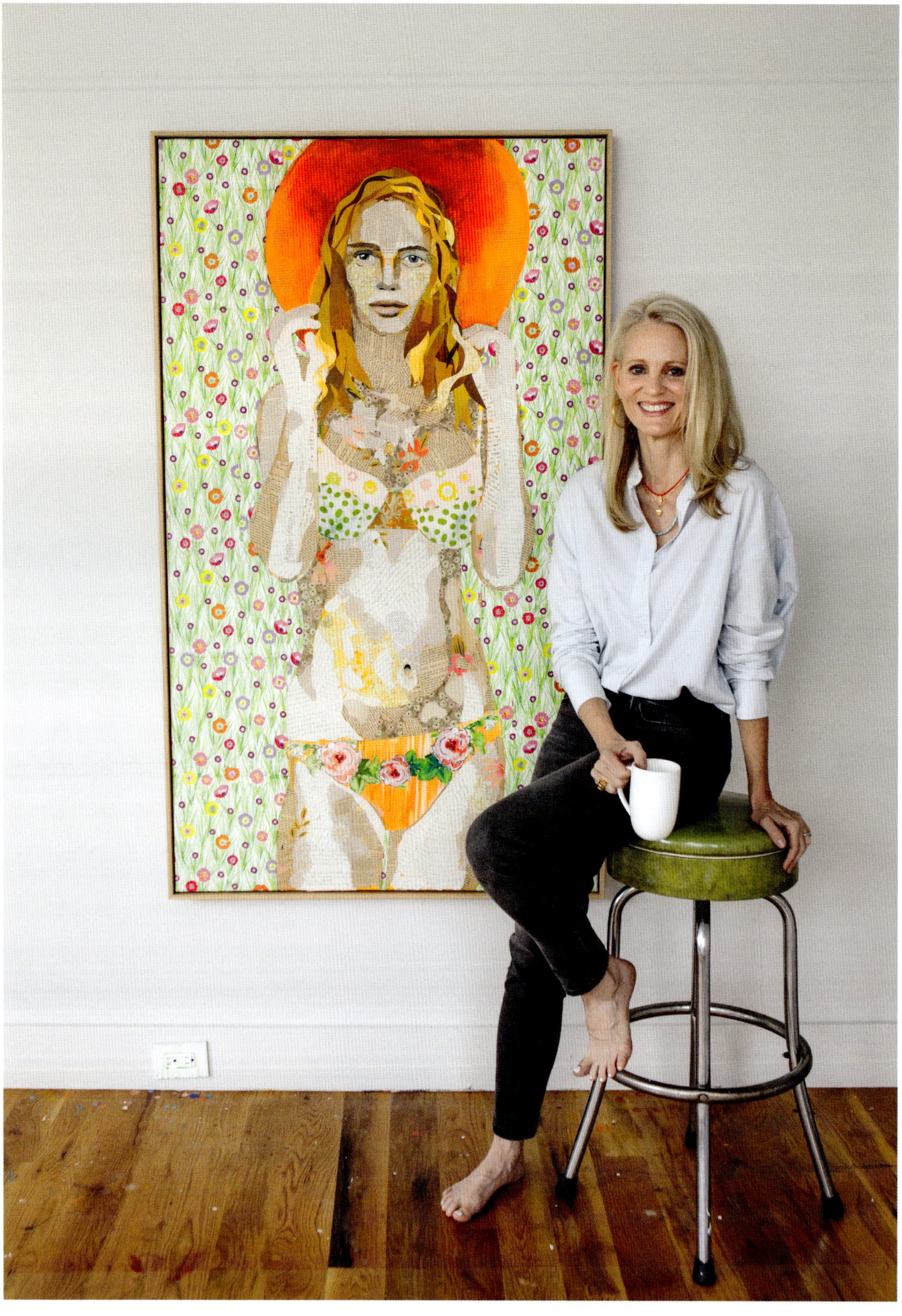

ABOUT THE AUTHOR

Brenda Bogart's Dallas studio is chockfull of boxes from literally everywhere containing found and collected objects that serve to inspire her next work of art. She defines collaging as painting with paper and coaxes this chaotic medium into an intriguing work of art using her distinct style of color, pattern, and texture.

She has been known to rescue trash out of a muddy puddle, along with countless other items on long walks with her husband and dogs. In fact, she was once almost arrested in front of the Supreme Court building in Washington, DC, when a piece of peeling paint on a public trash can caught her eye! A scary swarm of armed security officers quickly surrounded Brenda on bicycles, demanding she hand over the chunk of flakey paint. Brenda haunts the halls of Europe and the countryside flea markets of rural America for hand-lettered antique documents and paper ephemera to bring back to her Dallas studio.

Brenda earned a degree in Interior Design from Texas Christian University in Fort Worth. After a successful career as an interior designer, she began studying painting and drawing at Southern Methodist University extensively under Mary Vernon and Barnaby Fitzgerald. Brenda has two adult children, is a native Texan, and lives in Dallas, Texas, with her husband, Bill.

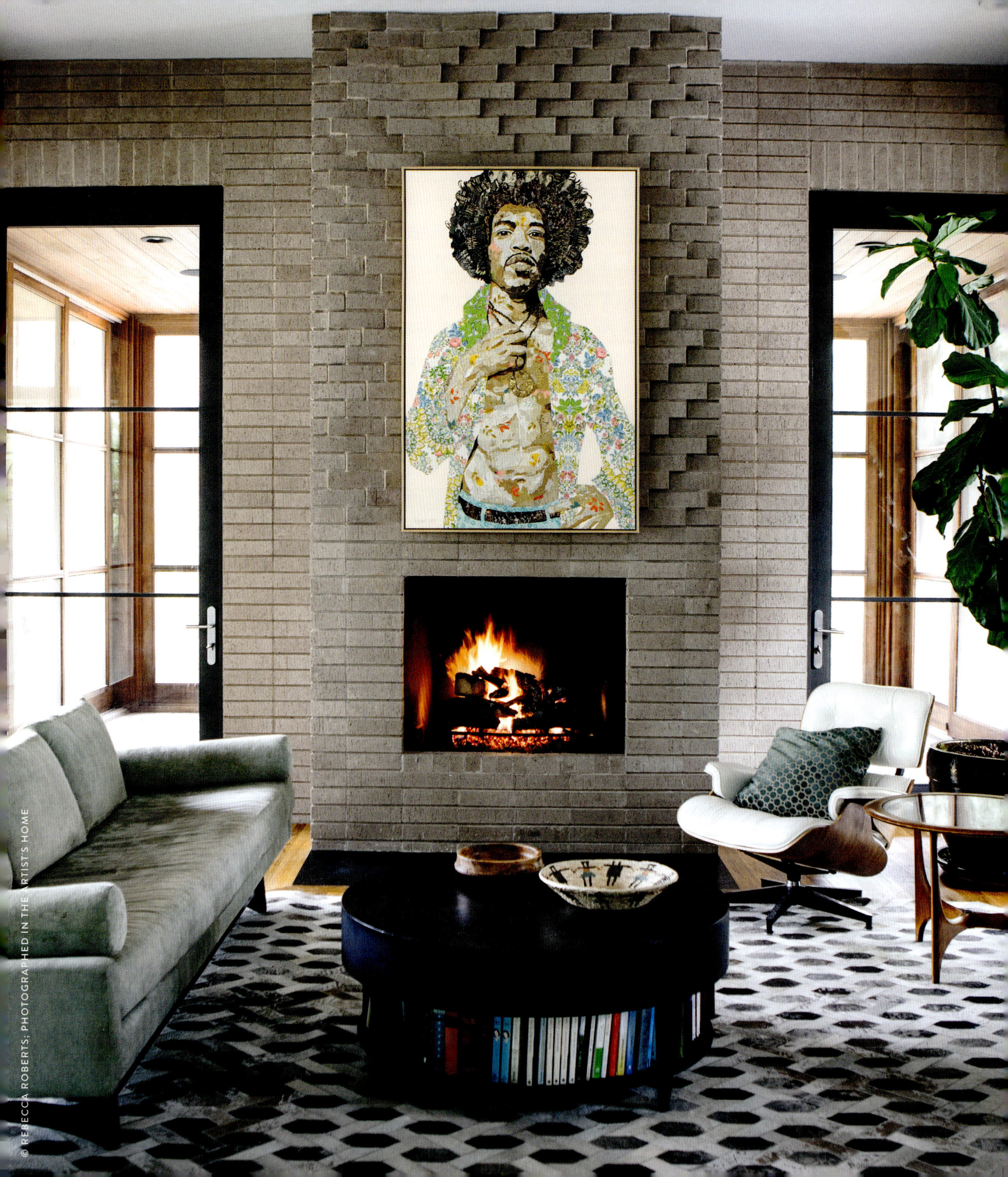

INTRODUCTION

First of all, *thank you* for picking up this book and enjoying the art, inspiration, and scriptures that mean so much to me.

The goal of this book is to highlight a 40-day season of Lent, an annual opportunity to focus our time and energy on something greater than ourselves. But it's also my desire that you feel free to use this book to inspire and encourage you anytime of the year. The themes are so common to everyday life that I hope they become something you can read over and over again.

Maybe you've never experienced the 40 days of Lent, an ancient Christian tradition that begins with Ash Wednesday and lasts through Easter Sunday. I like to think of Lent as a hard reset to spend more time in Scripture and more attention focusing on the priceless gift that Christ gave us through his sacrifice on the cross. It's a time for me to focus on the things I need to let go of so that I can gain more of what God wants me to have. Some people give up wine or chocolate during Lent. When I thought about giving up something more significant, I started to think about the deeper matters of the heart.

An intentional season like Lent separates our wants from our needs. The people who give regularly to others and to God's work are the happiest people I know. They're just the most joyful people to be around. And they aren't necessarily wealthy people. I know people who give to those who have lots more than they do. I love the idea of sacrifice because we live in a consumer culture, always seeming to need more and more and more. We constantly tell ourselves we need more stuff. I hate to say it, but several years ago I actually bought 10 pairs of new shoes for spring!

Why did I *do* that?

Lent is about breaking me-centered habits. It is a participatory practice that increases our awareness of the matchless sacrifice Christ made for us. Sacrifice should hurt a little, you know. Or else it's not really a sacrifice, is it? When we don't give much of anything away—our time, our resources—we risk turning into the moldy, water-soaked sponge in the bottom of the sink. I never get squeezed out if I don't give and if I don't sacrifice. We weren't designed to function well with the mindset of hoarding our gifts and keeping them all for ourselves. We were *created* to give. I like to say, "Give until it is lifestyle-altering." This applies to more than my checkbook. It includes an investment of my emotions, humility, submission, and time.

God is asking us to be a conduit to pour out his love to each other and the world. Knowing that he created us from "dirt," I like to think of myself as the mud vessel through which the wild river of his love flows. My hope is that the inspiration contained in these pages reminds you to receive his love—and give it away.

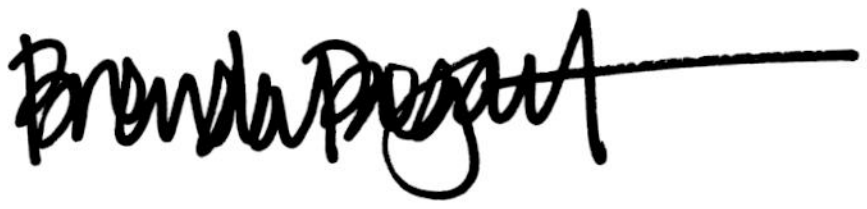

Dallas, Texas
Summer 2021

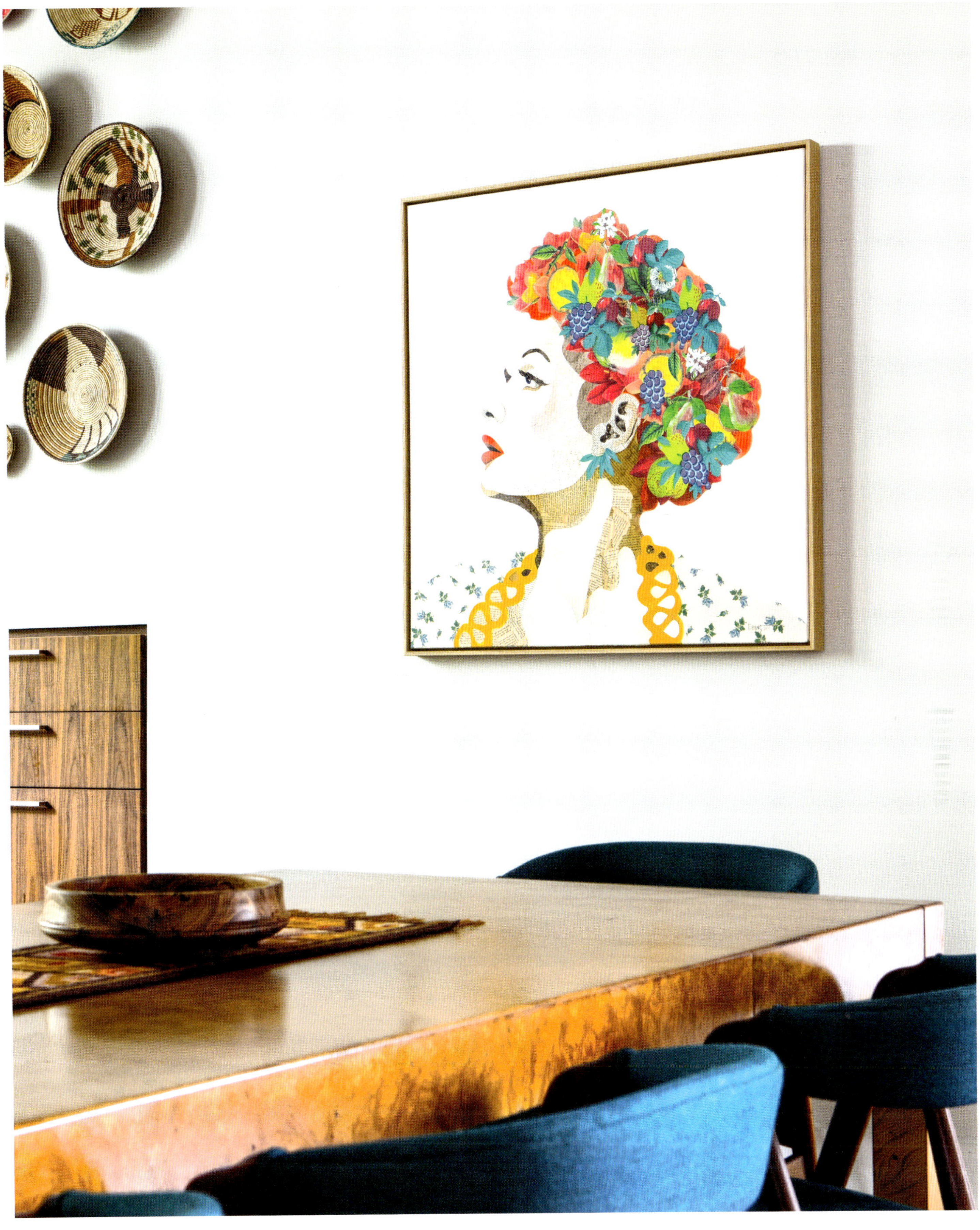

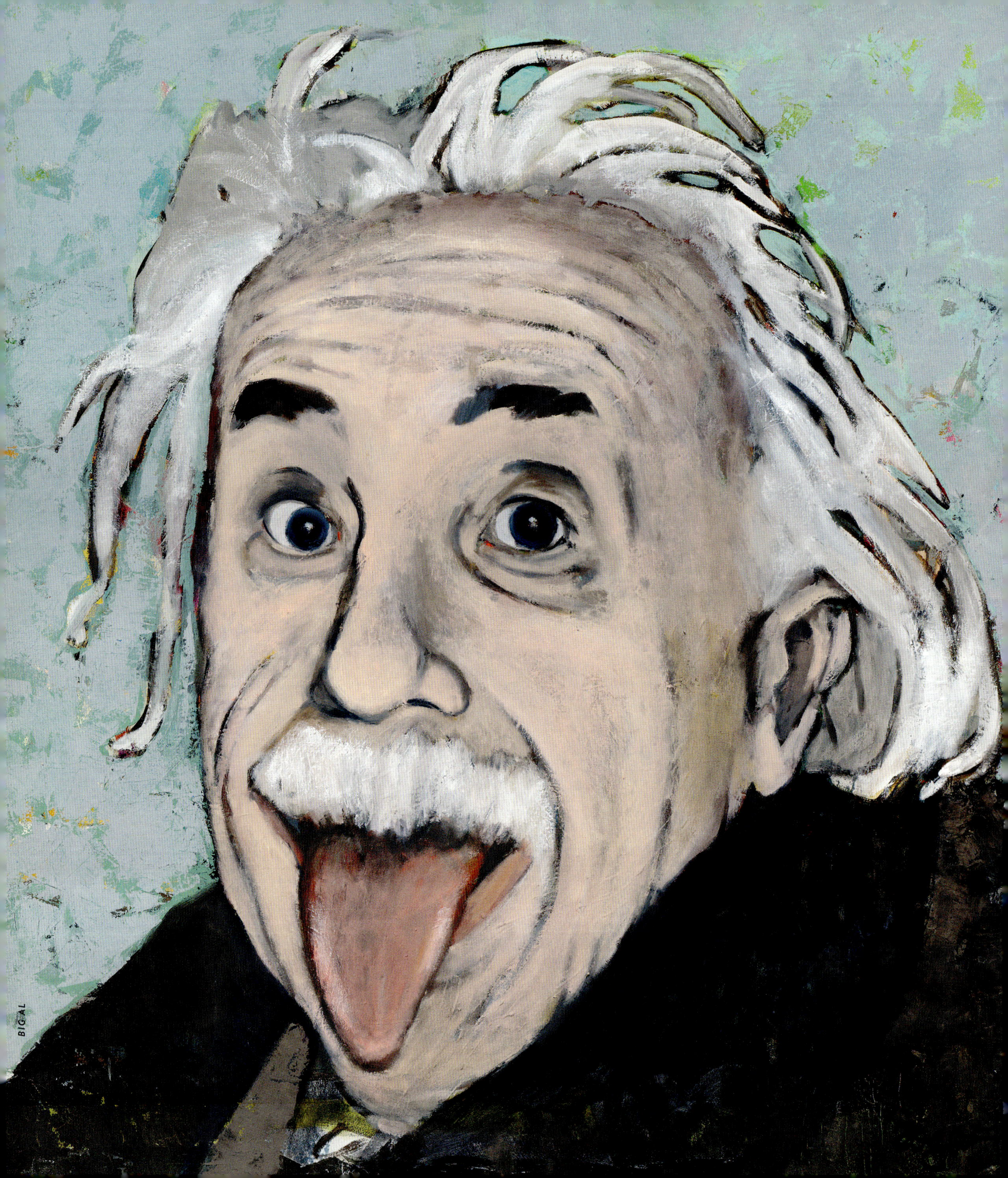
BIGAL

Day 1 • WHAT TO GIVE UP FOR LENT THAT'S NOT CHOCOLATE?

Taking Myself Too Seriously.

We were filled with laughter, and we sang for joy. And the other nations said, "What amazing things the Lord has done for them."

PSALM 126:2

Why do I feel like everything on my to-do list has to happen *today?*

My real job is to enjoy Jesus and to enjoy the life he's given me—not work myself into a frenzy. It seems that I'm often taking my life and myself too seriously.

When someone is enjoying God, what does that look like? For me, I'm in what I call "the flow." I love the flow. I'm in that relaxed, restful state and I'm doing the next thing because it's the next thing I feel called to do. And I do it because I want to—not because I'm working toward a deadline or in a hurry to get things done. I think of "the flow" as what the Bible calls being "in the Spirit," while "performance mode" is acting "in the flesh." When I get stuck in performance mode, it takes me out of the flow.

My engine tends to run hot, and it can make for an uncomfortable ride through life. Therefore, I work hard at relaxing. I do breathing exercises and talk to myself throughout the day, reminding myself to remain calm. The world in its foolishness tells us to work harder and do it all. When we take ourselves and our to-do lists less seriously, we stress less and learn to enjoy life the way God wants us to instead.

Stop deceiving yourselves. If you think you are wise by this world's standards, you need to become a fool to be truly wise. For the wisdom of this world is foolishness to God. As the Scriptures say, "He traps the wise in the snare of their own cleverness."

1 CORINTHIANS 3:18–19

He will wipe every tear from their eyes, and there will be no more death or sorrow or crying or pain. All these things are gone forever.

REVELATION 21:4

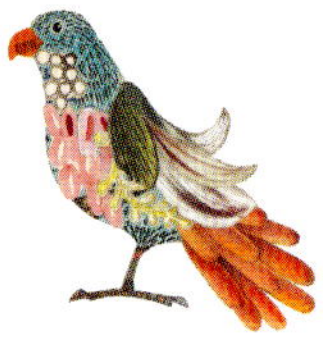

- What makes you anxious?
- What does your life look like when you are enjoying God?

May God give you a real and tangible sense of joy today.

A glad heart makes a happy face; a broken heart crushes the spirit.

PROVERBS 15:13

HAVING A COLD HEART.

But the Lord said to Samuel, "Don't judge by his appearance or height, for I have rejected him. The Lord doesn't see things the way you see them. People judge by outward appearance, but the Lord looks at the heart."

1 SAMUEL 16:7

This verse used to give me great comfort. But around my mid-thirties it hit me pretty hard that this was not so comforting. By that point, I was self-aware enough to examine the truth about my own heart: a heart that is stubborn to forgive, that holds onto bitterness and chews on offenses like a cow chewing cud.

And I was also old enough to know how easy it is to put on a good appearance. That is when a lifelong journey began for me of focusing on the condition of my heart. I'm still on that journey. The transformation is slow, and I have lots of relapses. But this is what I know: God loves me and my fickle heart. And I know that experiencing the love of God is what transforms a heart of stone into a heart of flesh.

The human heart is the most deceitful of all things, and desperately wicked. Who really knows how bad it is?

JEREMIAH 17:9

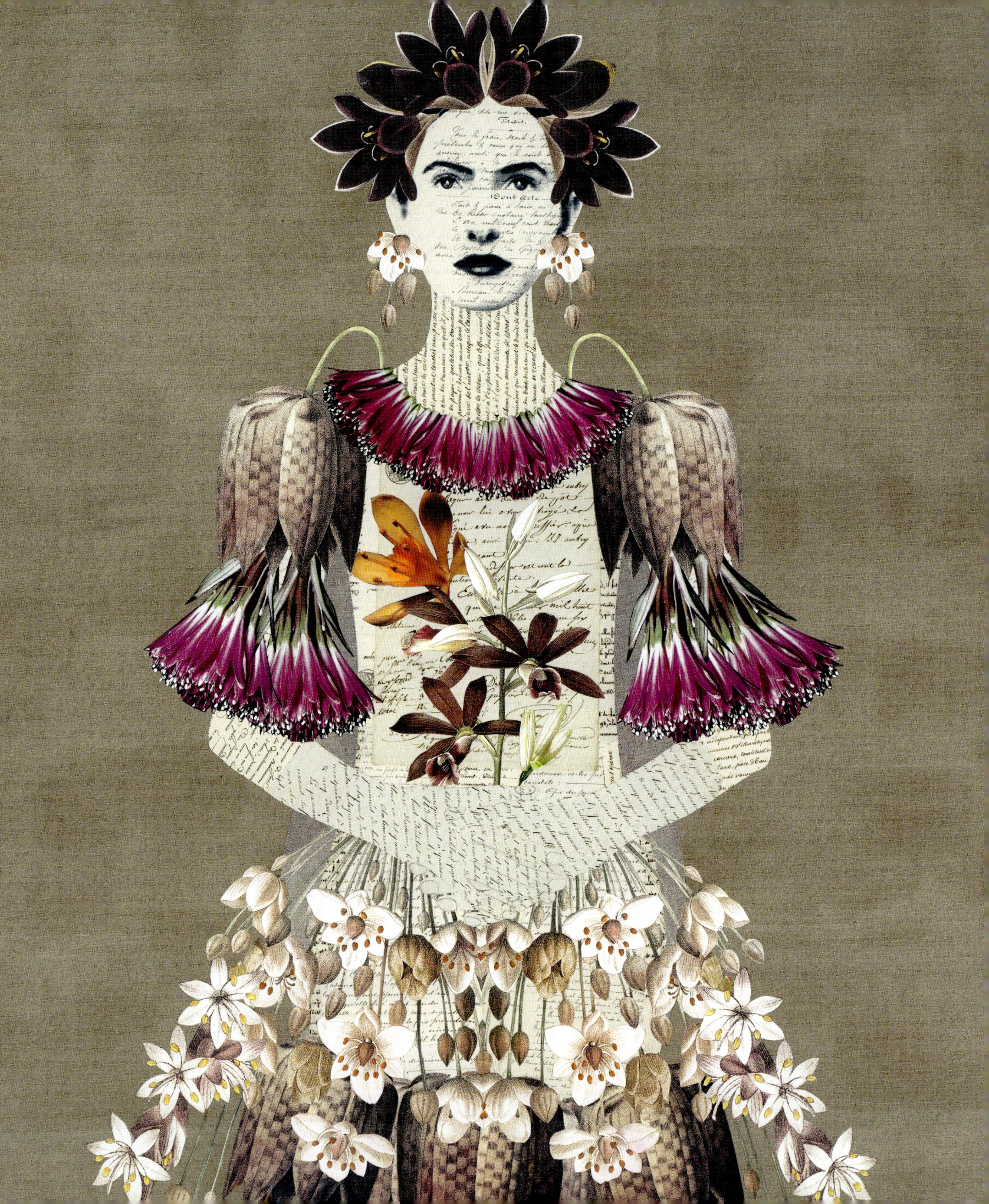

GARDEN QUEEN "PRIMROSE"

And I will give you a new heart, and I will put a new spirit in you. I will take out your stony, stubborn heart and give you a tender, responsive heart.

EZEKIEL 36:26

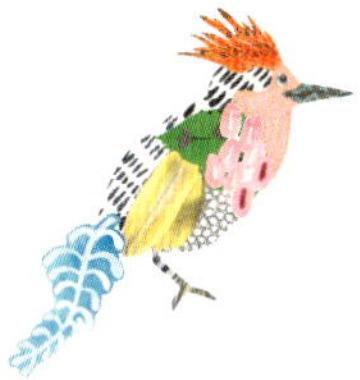

- How would you describe your journey of the heart these days?
- What are you learning about God's great love for you?

May God soften our hearts of stone and from them flow springs of life.

Keep your heart with all vigilance, for from it flow the springs of life.

PROVERBS 4:23

Your Comfort Zone.

The Lord had said to Abram, "Leave your native country, your relatives, and your father's family, and go to the land that I will show you. I will make you into a great nation. I will bless you and make you famous, and you will be a blessing to others. I will bless those who bless you and curse those who treat you with contempt. All the families on earth will be blessed through you."

GENESIS 12:1-3

Abram and Sarai had it pretty good in Haran. They had their family, friends, and extended relatives, and supposedly a comfortable home with indoor plumbing. If I had to boil it down to my two most basic comforts in life, it's those two things: the comfort of my loved ones and indoor plumbing.

But he left it all to live in the desert in a tent. And he was 75 years old!

When I was 45, at the height of my career, I felt God calling me to lay down my interior design business and pursue art full time. I didn't have a degree in art and had no clue what this was going to look like. Or if I could ever make a dime doing it. The call was so strong, however, I could not say no. Every day that I delayed felt as if I were walking through mud.

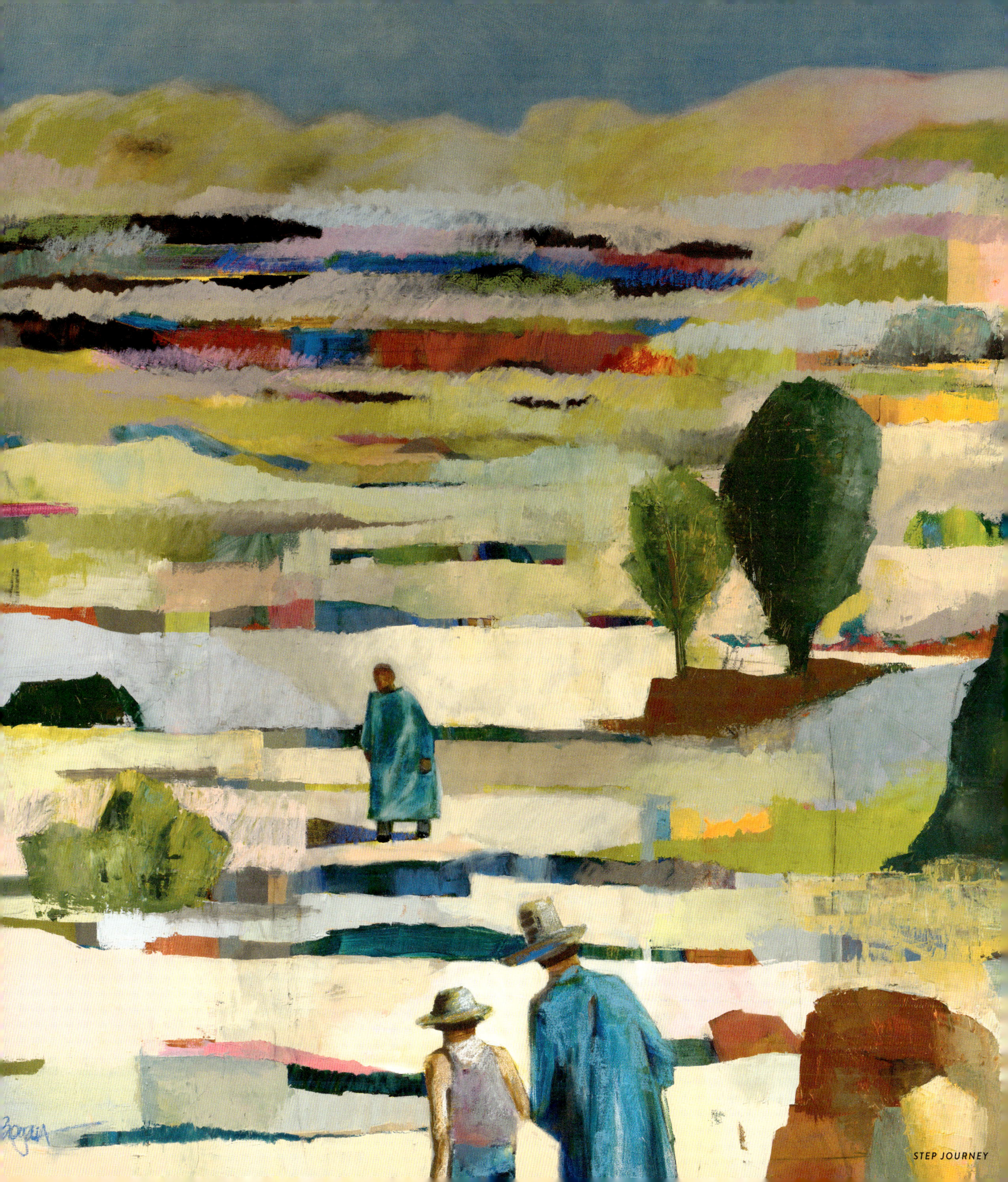

STEP JOURNEY

Fifteen years later I can tell you that some decisions are scary, and this was one of the best scary decisions I ever made! It has not been a straight line. There have been many highs and lows, but this has been the sweet spot of my life. What seemingly crazy thing is God calling you to do? I can promise it will be the ride of your life!

For the rest of the story on Abram, later named Abraham by God, start in Genesis 12 and keep reading...all the way through Revelation 22.

For I can do everything through Christ, who gives me strength.

PHILIPPIANS 4:13

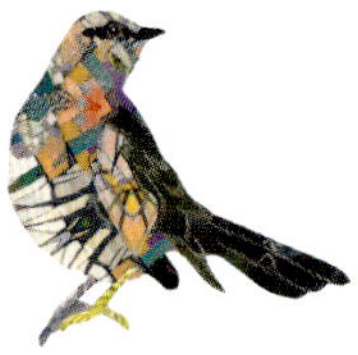

- What do you think you're really meant to be doing in this season of your life?
- What are some of the best scary decisions you've ever made?
- Why are some decisions harder to make than others?

May God lead you to whatever is next in your journey—
and may you have the faith to pursue it.

Seek his will in all you do, and he will show you which path to take.

PROVERBS 3:6

Obsessive People Pleasing.

This is what the Lord says: Cursed are those who put their trust in mere humans, who rely on human strength and turn their hearts away from the Lord. They are like stunted shrubs in the desert, with no hope for the future...But blessed are those who trust in the Lord and have made the Lord their hope and confidence. They are like trees planted along a riverbank, with roots that reach deep into the water. Such trees are not bothered by the heat or worried by long months of drought. Their leaves stay green, and they never stop producing fruit.

JEREMIAH 17:5–8

It has taken me a long time, but I have learned I must give up my need to please everyone. Obsessive people pleasing leaves me in a state of perpetual disappointment and a continuous circle of not measuring up. It's like laundry that never gets clean, no matter how many times you spin it through the cycles.

The only person I am to please is the Lord. When I look at the life of Jesus, I see a man who spent his days preaching God's Word and healing the sick, yet people were constantly disappointed in him. Some even wanted to kill him. One day I asked our pastor, Mark Davis, how he handles it if some people are displeased with his work. He replied, "All I know is that the best preacher who ever lived got hung on a tree."

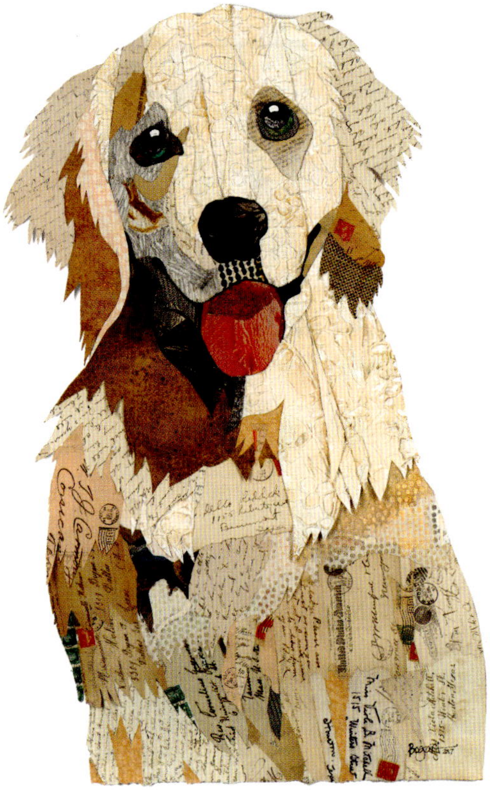

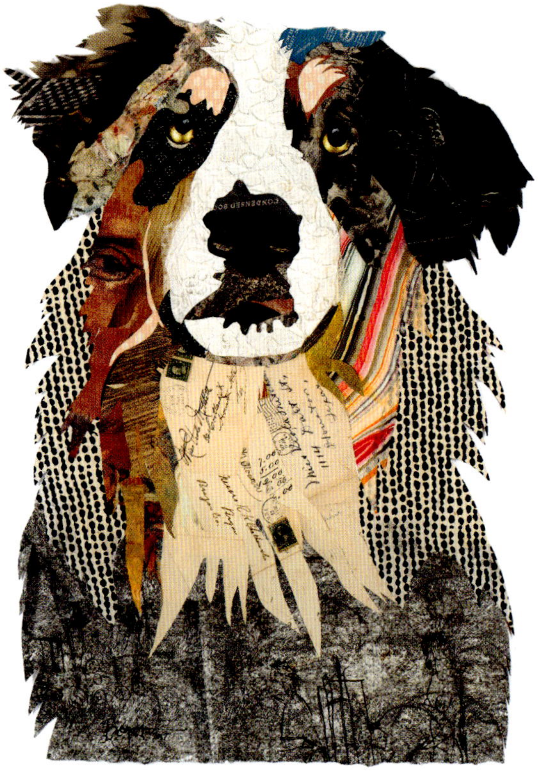

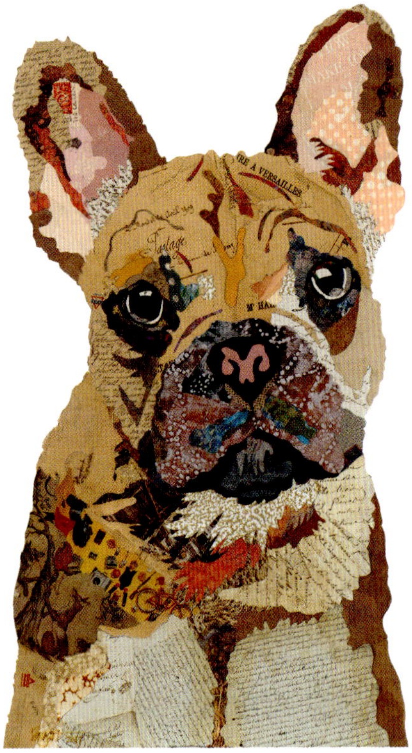

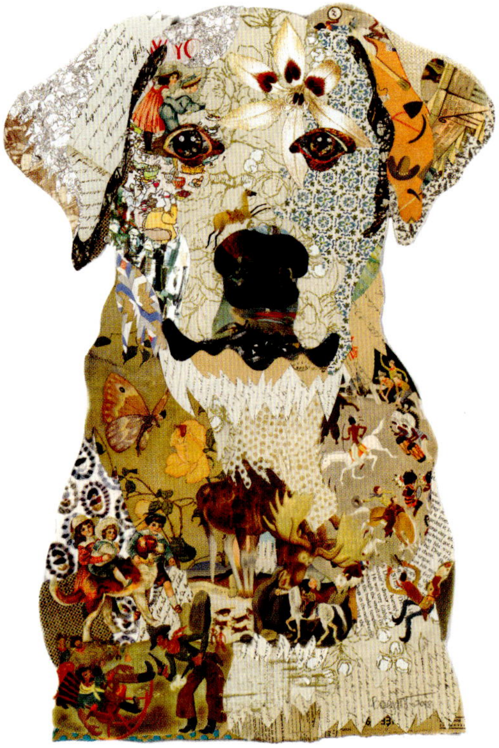

Pleasing others leads to confusion about our true path. If we are doing things right and what best fits our true path and purpose in life, there will be those who are disappointed in us. Our parents. Our friends. Our colleagues. But that's okay. It really is okay.

Obviously, I'm not trying to win the approval of people, but of God. If pleasing people were my goal, I would not be Christ's servant.

GALATIANS 1:10

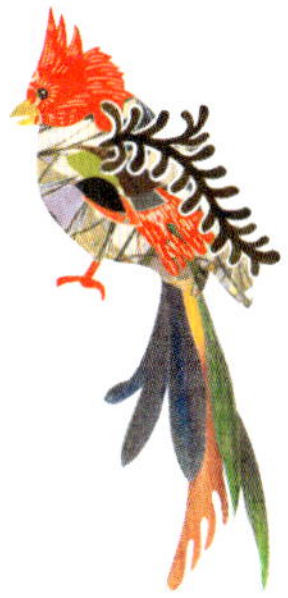

- When are you most tempted to arrange your life around pleasing others?
- Who do you most often turn to for approval?

May God lead you to experience the greater joy in pleasing only him.

And it is impossible to please God without faith.

HEBREWS 11:6

Withholding Love.

My beloved friends, let us continue to love each other since love comes from God. Everyone who loves is born of God and experiences a relationship with God. The person who refuses to love doesn't know the first thing about God, because God is love—so you can't know him if you don't love. This is how God showed his love for us: God sent his only Son into the world so we might live through him. This is the kind of love we are talking about—not that we once upon a time loved God, but that he loved us and sent his Son as a sacrifice to clear away our sins and the damage they've done to our relationship with God.

1 JOHN 4:7 MSG

When I am withholding love from someone, it is almost always because I am holding more tightly to a grudge. A grudge is just another word for unforgiveness. You know the saying—unforgiveness is like drinking poison and hoping the other person gets sick! It's true. Grudges hurt the grudge-holder. When I hold tightly to a grudge, I find it hard to feel light or happy. And I find it especially difficult to freely love the person I refuse to forgive.

Forgiveness is a daily practice. It's rarely one-and-done. But I can't dance in my heart

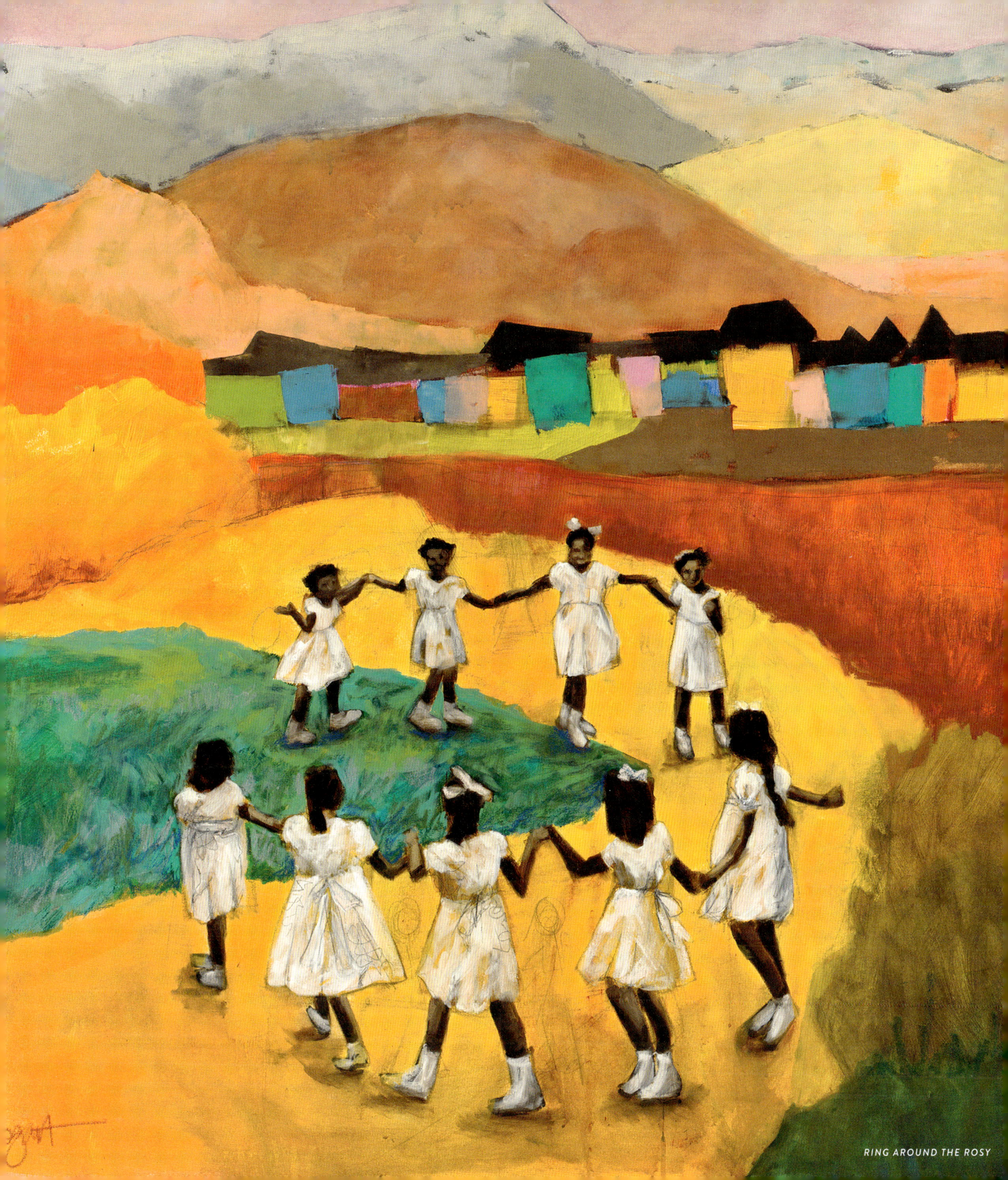

RING AROUND THE ROSY

like a child until I've released a grudge. Kindness is a practice also because harping on someone's faults is just fuel for a bitter heart. It creates estrangement and bitterness in our own hearts. When I get stuck and feel myself going the wrong way, I read over the fruit of the Spirit listed in Galatians 5. It's very practical and helps me to pinpoint where I might be withholding love from others. I ask myself: Where am I not being loving? Joyful? Peaceful? Patient? Kind? You get the idea.

I have found that the only way to accomplish effective change in my relationships is through love—loving God, loving others, loving myself, and acting in a loving way. Love conquers all.

Be kind to one another, tenderhearted, forgiving one another, as God in Christ forgave you.

EPHESIANS 4:32 ESV

Most important of all, continue to show deep love for each other, for love covers a multitude of sins.

1 PETER 4:8

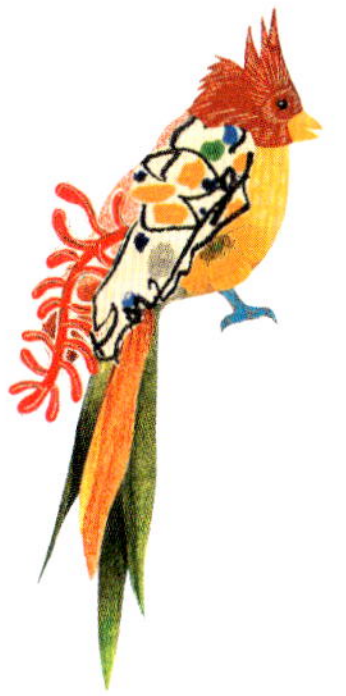

- When was the last time you held a grudge against someone? What did this accomplish?
- How does it feel to finally let go of a grudge and forgive?

May God loosen your grip on a grudge and help you let go.

But anyone who does not love does not know God, for God is love.

1 JOHN 4:8

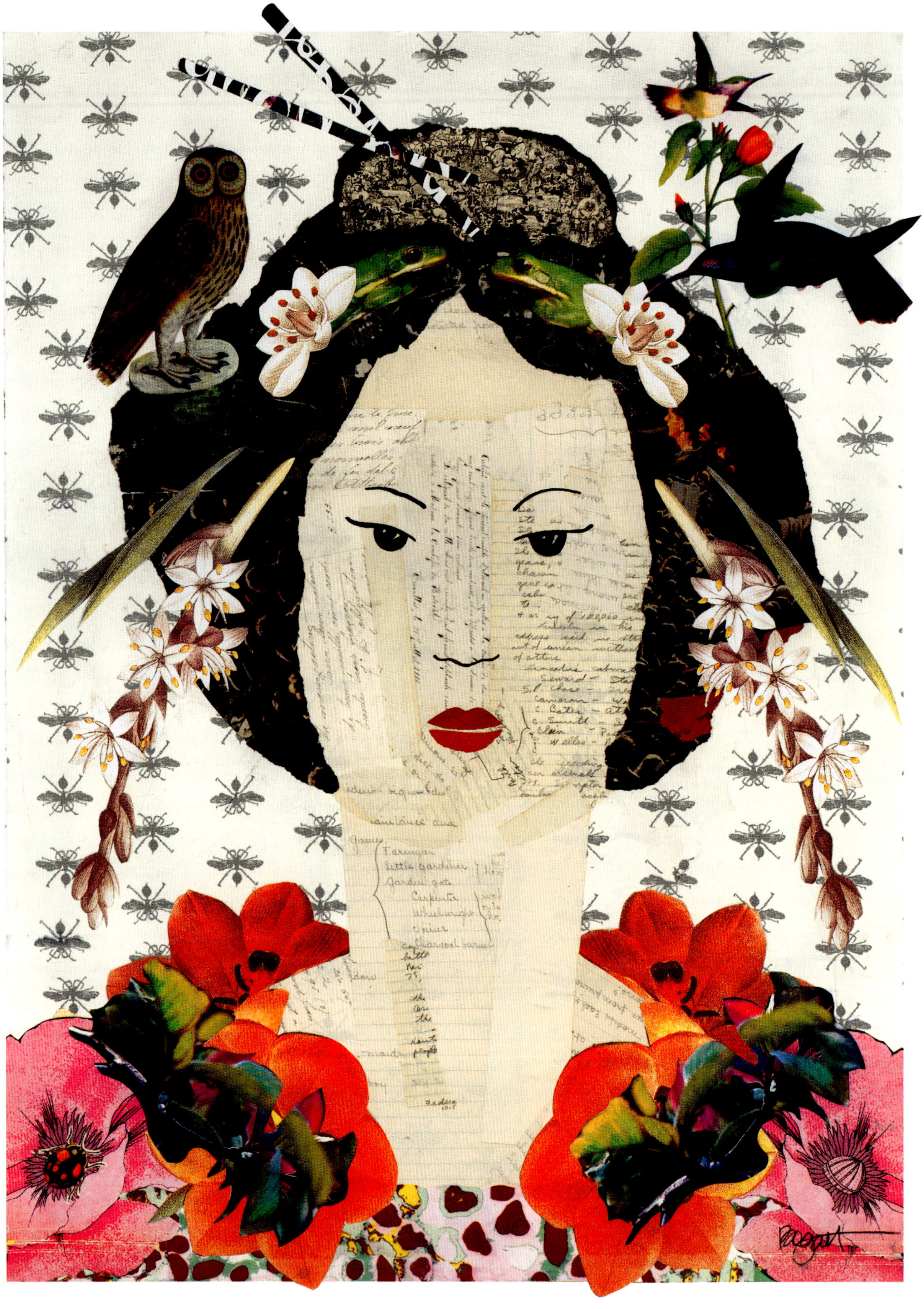

PERSEPHONE (GEISHA GIRLS)

Day 6 • WHAT TO GIVE UP FOR LENT THAT'S NOT CHOCOLATE?

HYPOCRISY.

For everyone has sinned; we all fall short of God's glorious standard. Yet God, in his grace, freely makes us right in his sight. He did this through Christ Jesus when he freed us from the penalty for our sins. For God presented Jesus as the sacrifice for sin. People are made right with God when they believe that Jesus sacrificed his life, shedding his blood. This sacrifice shows that God was being fair when he held back and did not punish those who sinned in times past. Can we boast, then, that we have done anything to be accepted by God? No, because our acquittal is not based on obeying the law. It is based on faith. So we are made right with God through faith and not by obeying the law. There is only one God, and he makes people right with himself only by faith, whether they are Jews or Gentiles.

ROMANS 3:23–25, 27–28, 30

Christians are just saved sinners.

When we expect Christians to set a better example, it's understandable. But it's also like expecting an acorn to resemble an oak tree. Salvation is a gift that is received; no one earns it—not even the best Christian. If Christians' hypocrisy has kept you from coming to God, look to Christ, not other Christians, as your example to follow.

If you're the one guilty of hypocrisy, ask for God's help to be more authentic.

Remember, it is not by our good deeds that we are saved. It is impossible to earn our salvation. Instead, God declares us righteous through faith in Jesus Christ's substitutionary death for our sins. That's a once-and-for-all act.

But, sadly, it doesn't mean we will always act righteous. Only God is truly righteous.

Jesus told him, "I am the way, the truth, and the life.
No one can come to the Father except through me."

JOHN 14:6

God saved you by his grace when you believed. And you can't take credit for this; it is a gift from God.

EPHESIANS 2:8

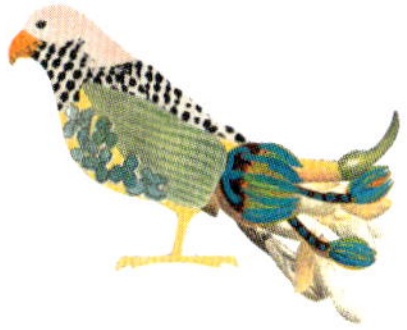

- Why do people think they have to earn their salvation?
- What do you appreciate the most about grace?

Let it sink in—God loves you (and everyone else) as you are, not as you should be.

But God showed his great love for us by sending Christ to die for us while we were still sinners.

ROMANS 5:8

Entitlement.

Now such persons we command and encourage in the Lord Jesus Christ to do their work quietly and to earn their own living.

2 THESSALONIANS 3:12 ESV

Ouch! But isn't this your worst pet peeve? Witnessing the entitlement in others? We can see it so clearly then. I can almost hear fingernails scratching down the chalkboard. It is that annoying! But do I see this in myself? For today, I am asking God to gently show *me* where I am feeling and acting entitled. Even in the littlest of ways. Show me, Lord, so I can confess and change my ways.

For instance, do I feel rules that apply to others don't apply to me? Do I dominate conversations and expect others to be more interested in me than I am in them? Am I easily offended when someone deviates from my personal list of rules about the right way to do everything? Do I cancel appointments at the last minute without regard to the inconvenience this places on others?

Am I slow to return something I have borrowed? Am I easily offended when I am not properly thanked or appreciated? Do I feel annoyed when people ask me for small favors? Well, I could go on, but you get the idea. This is just the start of my

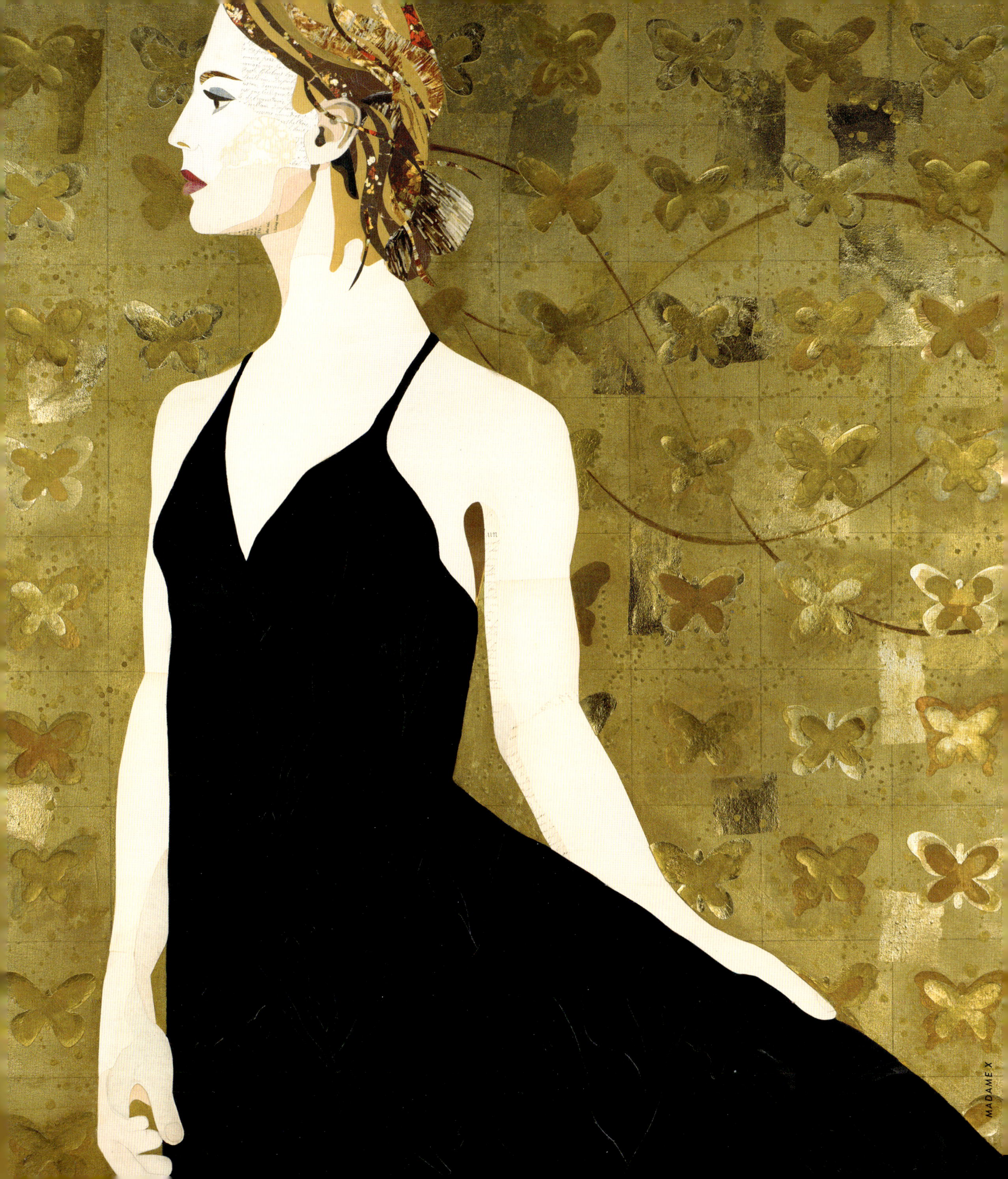
MADAME X

list. I am not beating myself up over these things. I just want to be more self-aware so I will be better and do better. I am praying I will be more annoyed with my own entitlement than other people's—so much so that I will not even notice theirs.

If you also wrestle with this, you are not alone!

> *What is causing the quarrels and fights among you? Don't they come from the evil desires at war within you? You want what you don't have, so you scheme and kill to get it. You are jealous of what others have, but you can't get it, so you fight and wage war to take it away from them. Yet you don't have what you want because you don't ask God for it. And even when you ask, you don't get it because your motives are all wrong—you want only what will give you pleasure.*
>
> **JAMES 4:1-3**

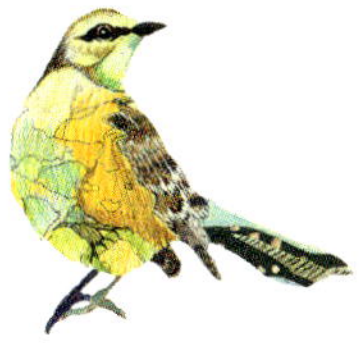

- What is your definition of "entitlement"?
- What are your personal struggles with entitlement—large and small?

May God bless you with feeling blessed, rather than feeling entitled.

Whatever is good and perfect is a gift coming down to us from God our Father, who created all the lights in the heavens.

JAMES 1:17

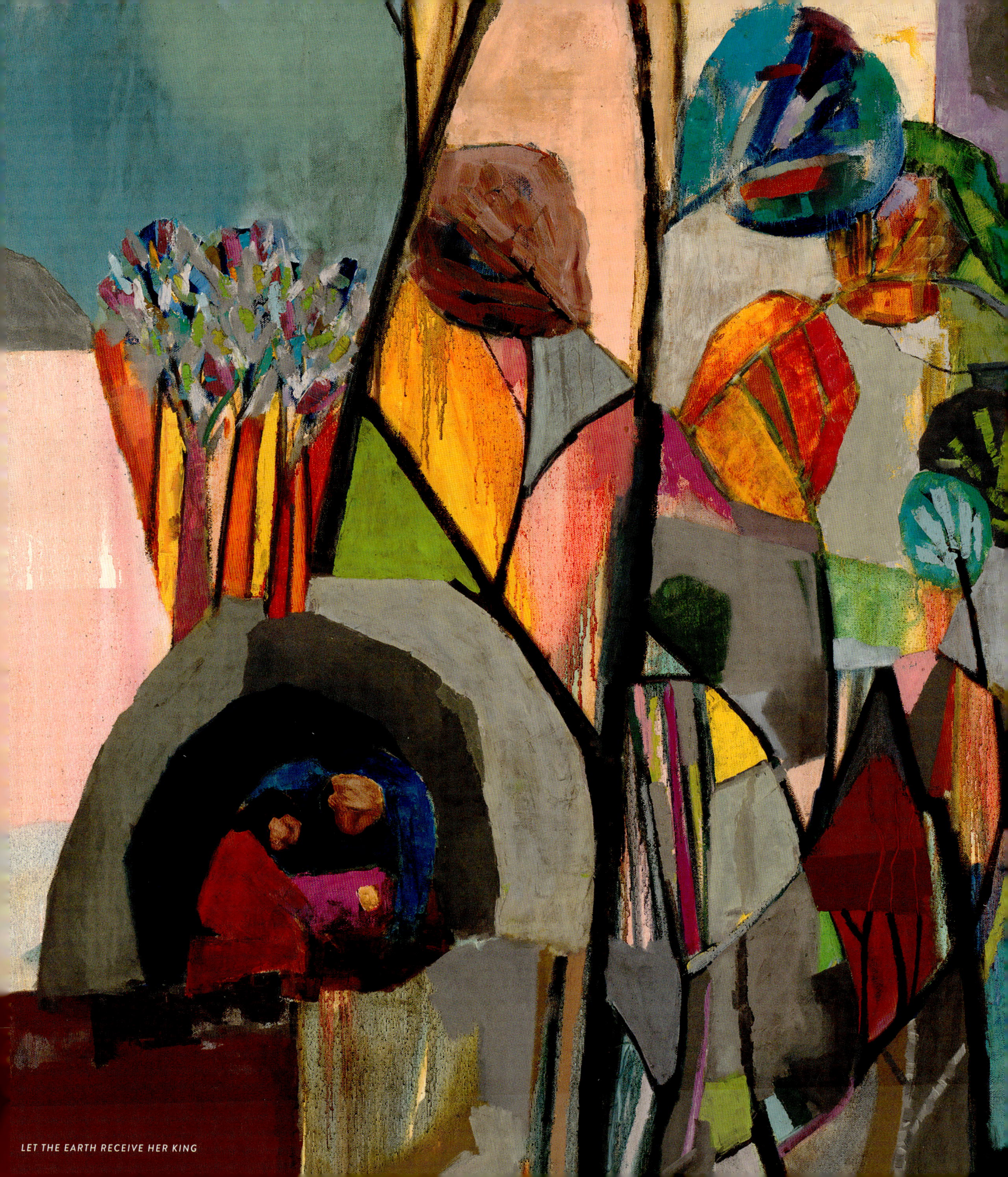

LET THE EARTH RECEIVE HER KING

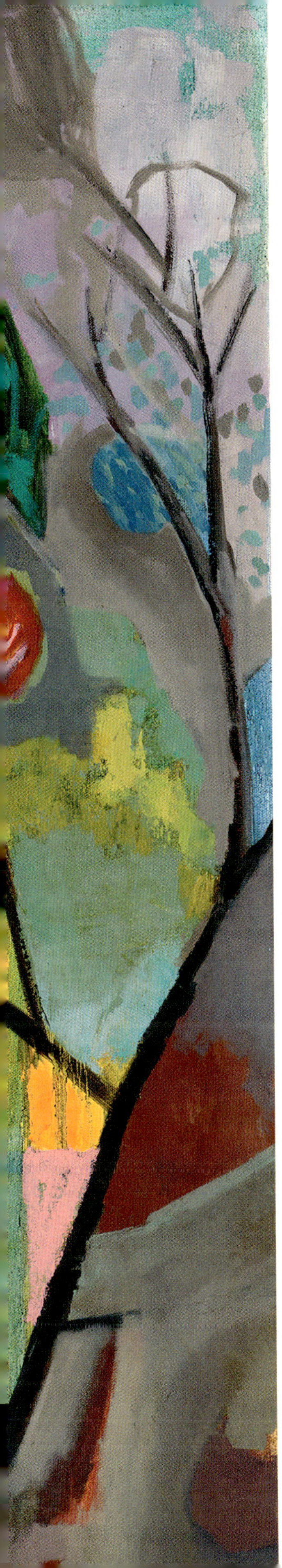

Rejecting Our True Light.

For it is you who lights my lamp; the Lord my God lightens my darkness.

PSALM 18:28 ESV

I will never forget driving the backroads alone in the dark on my way down to San Antonio from Fort Worth. There are barely any towns, no streetlights, and many miles between gas stations. The night was black as black could be. Gripping the steering wheel, I was so afraid something bad might happen. What would I do? Who could help me? It did not help matters that I was also going through a dark time in my life and some uncomfortable decisions awaited me.

I was in a valley of darkness, in more ways than one.

Suddenly a golden light from the rising moon illuminated the empty passenger seat beside me. The moonlight stayed with me the rest of the trip, never even hiding behind a cloud. I knew I was not alone. God was holding me. He lit the way before me, and I no longer had reason to fear. The light was so bright, like a beam from a flashlight, and I arrived in San Antonio safely that night unharmed. Not only that, but God also eventually guided my heart out of the darkness into the light again.

Whenever I experience a season of darkness or fear, that is when I can see God shine the brightest. It's like entering contrasting worlds, where my fear makes God's protection stand out even more. It causes me to remember that it was from utter darkness that God first spoke light into the world. Rejecting God, the true Light, means we choose to remain in darkness and fear on our scariest journeys. Instead, we can look for the light of his love to lead us all the way home.

> *And God said, "Let there be light," and there was light. And God saw that the light was good. And God separated the light from the darkness. God called the light Day, and the darkness he called Night. And there was evening and there was morning, the first day.*
>
> **GENESIS 1:3-5**

> *And night will be no more. They will need no light of lamp or sun, for the Lord God will be their light, and they will reign forever and ever.*
>
> **REVELATION 22:5 ESV**

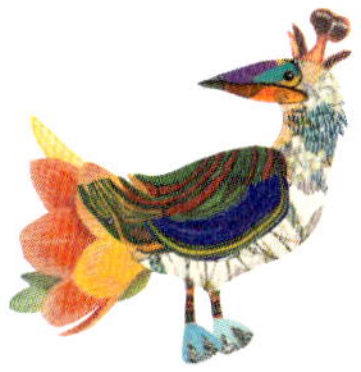

- Why is light a good description for God?
- When was a time that God's light shined the way for you in the darkness?

May God show you today that he is the source of all light, the One True Light.

Your word is a lamp to my feet and a light to my path.

PSALM 119:105

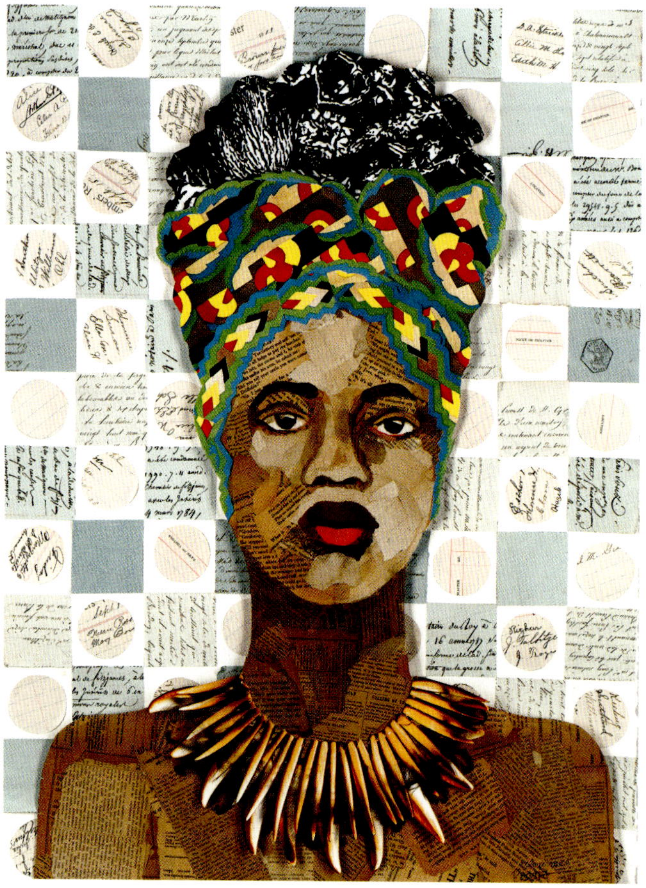

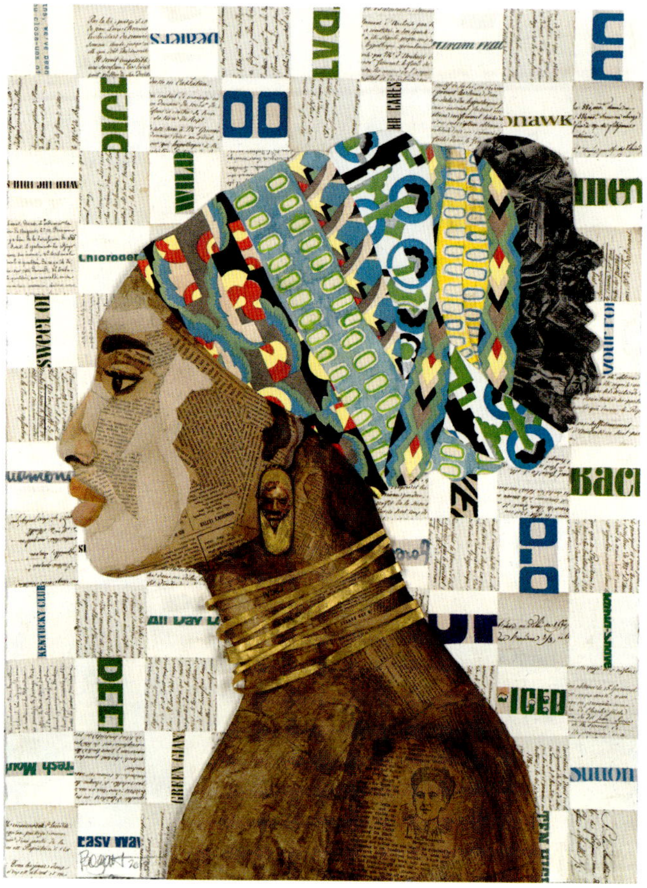

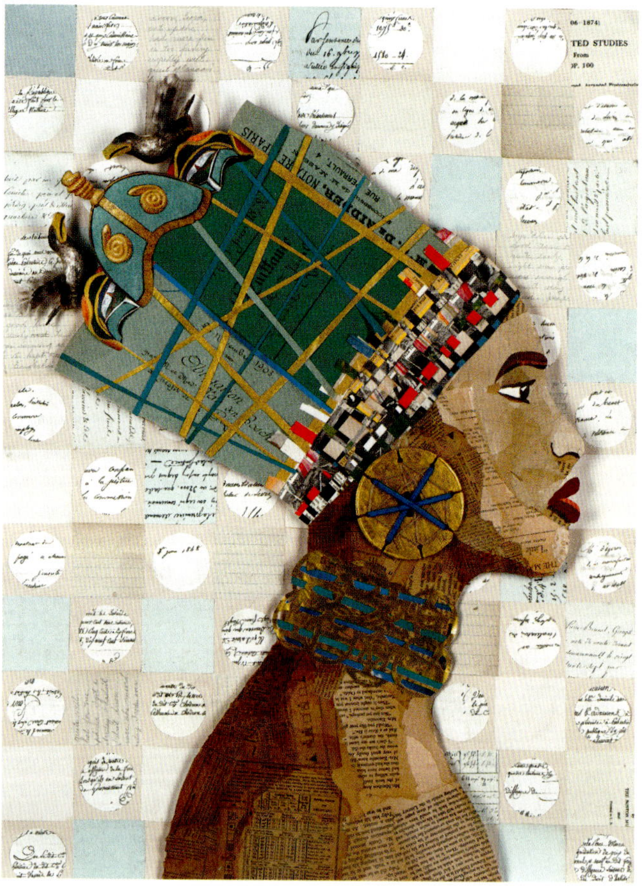

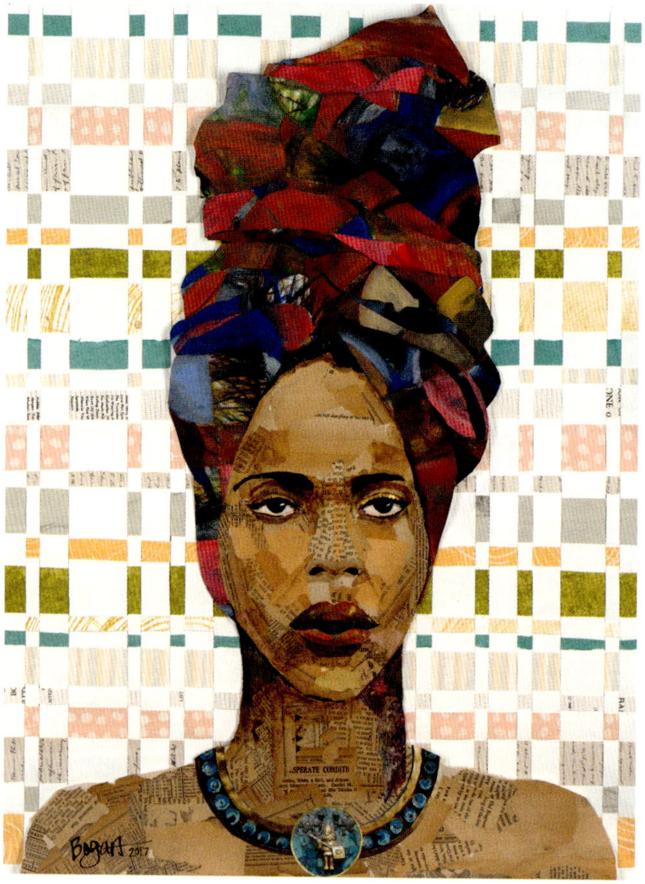

COMPOSURE, FAITHFULNESS, JOY, KINDNESS (AFRICAN QUEENS)

CRAVING THE NEXT GIFT.

Whom have I in heaven but you? I desire you more than anything on earth. My health may fail, and my spirit may grow weak, but God remains the strength of my heart; he is mine forever. Those who desert him will perish, for you destroy those who abandon you. But as for me, how good it is to be near God! I have made the Sovereign Lord my shelter, and I will tell everyone about the wonderful things you do.

PSALM 73:25-28

I do crave the next big "thing"—the intense pursuit of the next self-pleasure to lift my spirits. Sometimes it's retail therapy online. Sometimes it's getting a little something for my house. Sometimes it's reaching the next level of success or recognition. And sometimes it's planning a dream vacation or getaway. I am even guilty of planning my next adventure while I am still on the current one!

In these times, I find myself living gift to gift, always needing something to look forward to. Gifts are good at the time, but then "poof," the sense of satisfaction vanishes. Like most people, I want what I want, when I want it. But on a much deeper level I want to be so satisfied by God that I desire him more than anything this world has to offer. When I intentionally engage God through prayer and reading

Scripture, it causes me to want more of him and ignites a desire for the one thing that satisfies me most. The Bible talks about craving. Throughout the psalms, the writer says he longs for God with a deep hunger and thirst. Psalm 73 reminds me to be so dependent on and satisfied with the Giver of all good things that I do not crave the next gift.

Many people wake up wanting to tickle their brain right away in the morning with a routine like reading the news or scrolling through social media. My prayer most evenings before I go to sleep is, "Lord, wake me to want you!"

> *O God, you are my God; I earnestly search for you. My soul thirsts for you; my whole body longs for you in this parched and weary land where there is no water.*
>
> **PSALM 63:1 ESV**

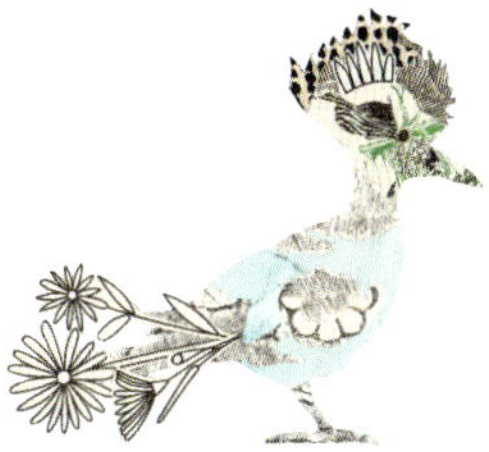

- What would you say is your deepest desire in all of life?
- What does it mean to be satisfied with God as the Giver, instead of wanting more gifts?

May God shift our hearts back to him as our primary craving.

My heart has heard you say, "Come and talk with me."
And my heart responds, "Lord, I am coming."

PSALM 27:8

Worrying That God Won't Provide.

Then, turning to his disciples, Jesus said, "That is why I tell you not to worry about everyday life—whether you have enough food to eat or enough clothes to wear. For life is more than food, and your body more than clothing. Look at the ravens. They don't plant or harvest or store food in barns, for God feeds them. And you are far more valuable to him than any birds! Can all your worries add a single moment to your life? And if worry can't accomplish a little thing like that, what's the use of worrying over bigger things?"

LUKE 12:22-26

Worry is when we find ourselves thinking about something for way too long—especially something over which we have no control. Meditating on our problems, instead of trusting, is worry. God's going to take care of it the way God's going to take care of it. Whether it's the way I want him to or not, God's will will prevail. I shouldn't waste my brain cells on worry.

But I do. How about you?

The smallest of creatures don't worry about where their food is coming from. And they don't have a home with a roof over their heads. We have so much. And God

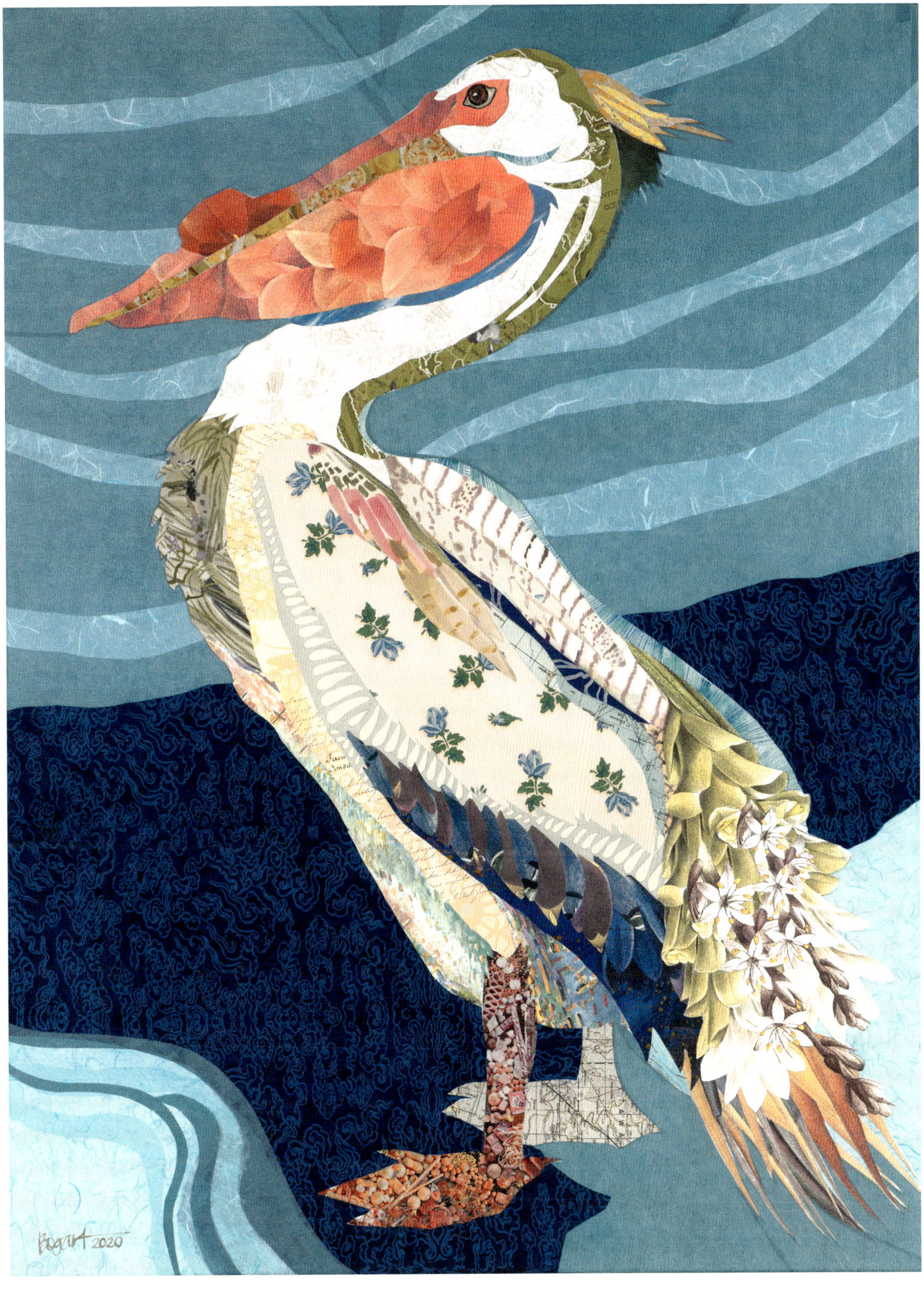

PELICAN 1

provided all of it. When we depend too much on ourselves, we tend to forget this truth. Sometimes I even start to think I'm the provider. But God is the only true provider.

The eyes of all look to you in hope; you give
them their food as they need it.
When you open your hand, you satisfy the
hunger and thirst of every living thing.

PSALM 145:15-16

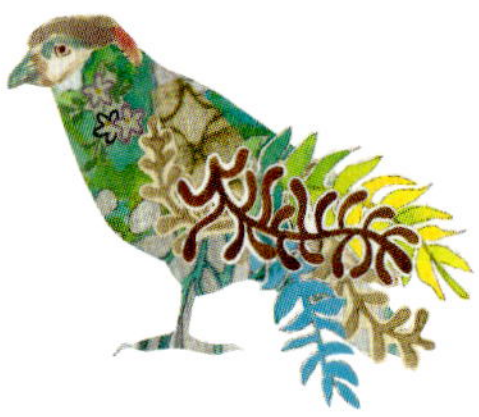

- What is worrying you right now?
- How can you give this concern over to God instead?

May you have faith today to turn over your worries to the God who loves you.

Give all your worries and cares to God, for he cares about you.

1 PETER 5:7

Doubting God's Sovereignty.

Who is this that questions my wisdom with such ignorant words? Brace yourself like a man, because I have some questions for you, and you must answer them. Where were you when I laid the foundations of the earth? Tell me, if you know so much. Who determined its dimensions and stretched out the surveying line? What supports its foundations, and who laid its cornerstone as the morning stars sang together and all the angels shouted for joy? Who kept the sea inside its boundaries as it burst from the womb, and as I clothed it with clouds and wrapped it in thick darkness? For I locked it behind barred gates, limiting its shores. I said, "This far and no farther will you come. Here your proud waves must stop!" Have you ever commanded the morning to appear and caused the dawn to rise in the east? Have you made daylight spread to the ends of the earth, to bring an end to the night's wickedness? As the light approaches, the earth takes shape like clay pressed beneath a seal; it is robed in brilliant colors. Have you visited the storehouses of the snow or seen the storehouses of hail? I have reserved them as weapons for the time of trouble, for the day of battle and war. Where is the path to the source of light? Where is the home of the east wind? Who created a channel for the torrents of rain? Who laid out the path for the lightning? Who makes the rain fall on barren land, in a desert where no one lives? Who sends rain to satisfy the parched ground and make the tender grass spring up? Does the rain have a father? Who gives birth to the dew? Who is the mother of the ice? Who gives birth to the frost from the heavens? For the water turns to ice as hard as rock, and the surface of the water freezes. Can you direct the movement of the stars—binding the cluster of the Pleiades or loosening the cords of Orion? Can you direct the constellations through the seasons or guide the Bear with her cubs across the heavens? Do you know the laws of the universe? Can you use them to regulate the earth? Can you shout to the clouds and make it rain? Can you make lightning appear and cause it to strike as you direct? Who gives intuition to the heart and instinct to the mind? Who is wise enough to count all the clouds? Who can tilt the water jars of heaven when the parched ground is dry and the soil has hardened into clods? Can you stalk prey for a lioness and satisfy the young lions' appetites as they lie in their dens or crouch in the thicket? Who provides food for the ravens when their young cry out to God and wander about in hunger?

EXCERPTS FROM JOB 38

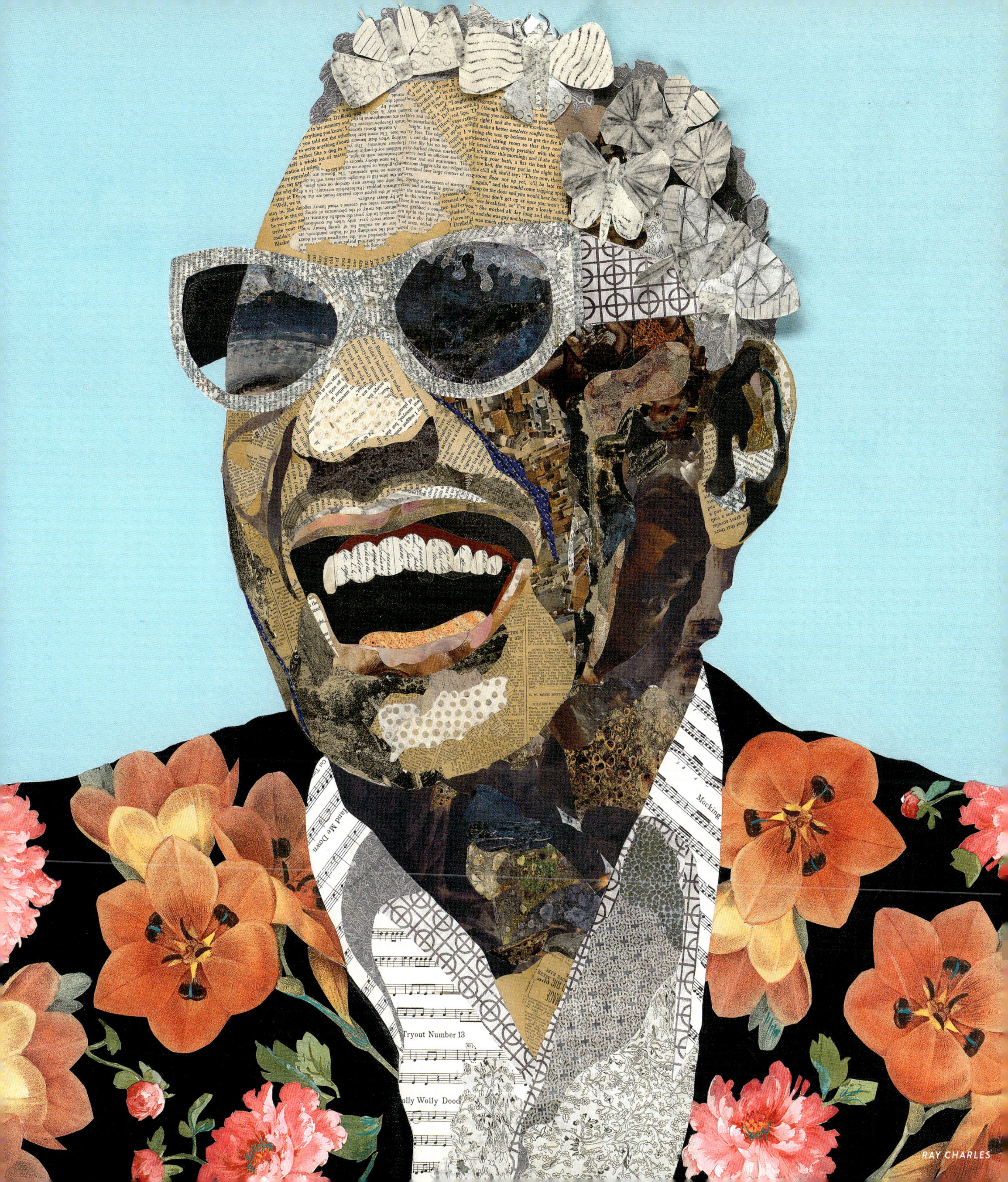

RAY CHARLES

Now that's a smack down!

In all of scripture, this powerful chapter in the Book of Job grips me like nothing else. It is both humbling and awe-inspiring. Like a splash of cold water, I am brought back to the center of what is real, taking away my haughtiness, pride, and fears.

What do you think of when you read these ancient words?

> *For who is God except the Lord? Who but our God is a solid rock? God is my strong fortress, and he makes my way perfect.*
>
> **2 SAMUEL 22:32-33**

> *Jesus replied, "Your mistake is that you don't know the Scriptures, and you don't know the power of God."*
>
> **MATTHEW 22:29**

> *Yours, O Lord, is the greatness, the power, the glory, the victory, and the majesty. Everything in the heavens and on earth is yours, O Lord, and this is your kingdom. We adore you as the one who is over all things.*
>
> **1 CHRONICLES 29:11**

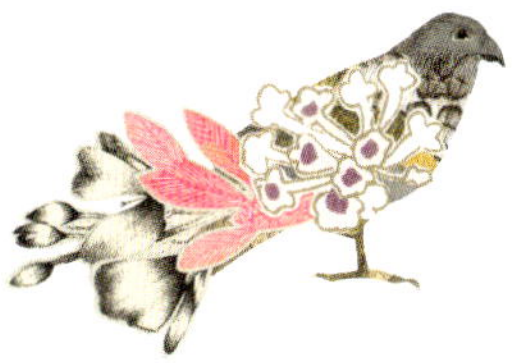

- Is there anything too difficult for God?
- What do you think it means for God's power to bring us "back to the center of what is real"?

Today, think big!
The whole power of God is available to you.

Now all glory to God, who is able, through his mighty power at work within us, to accomplish infinitely more than we might ask or think.

EPHESIANS 3:20

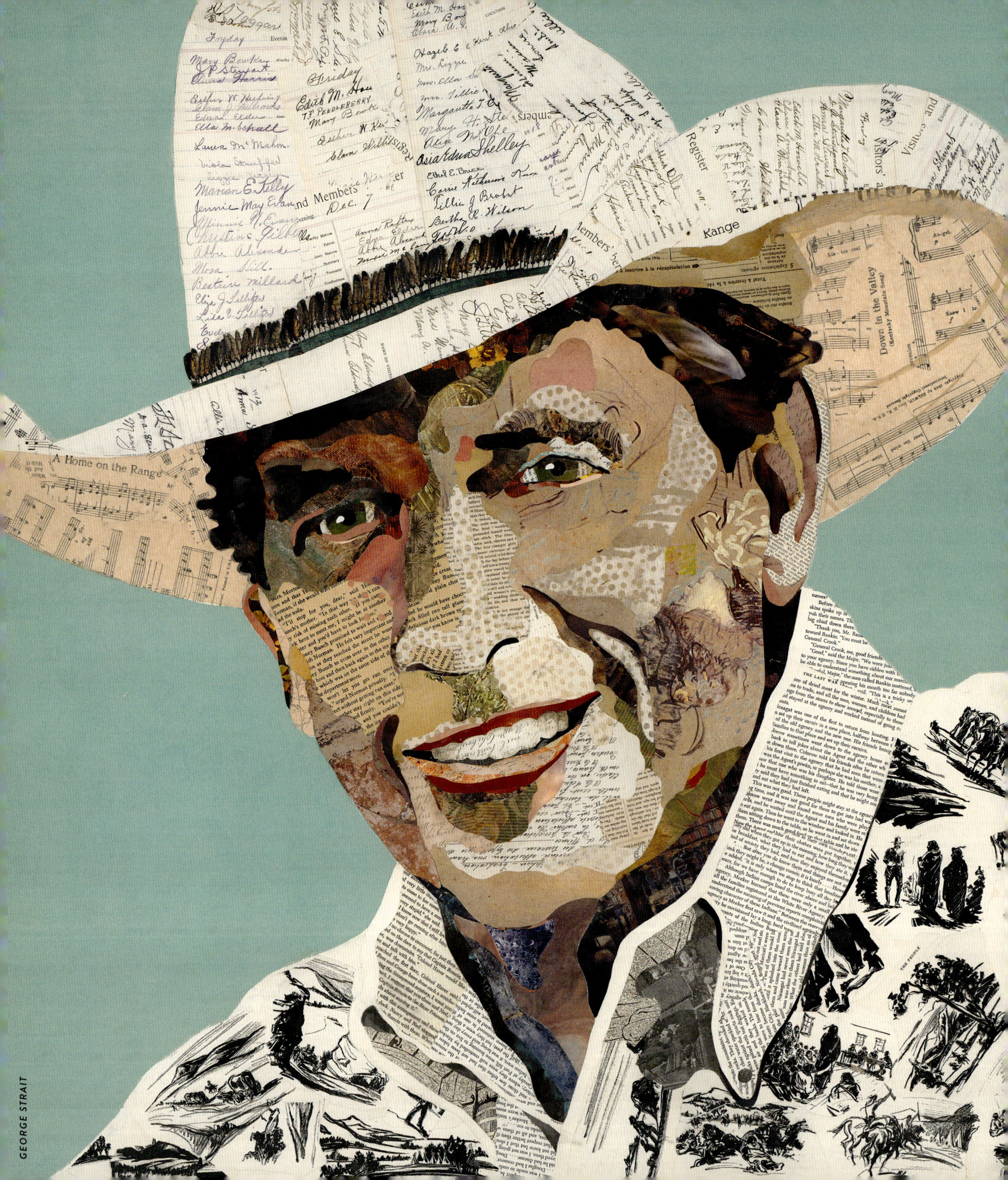

GEORGE STRAIT

LIVING A LIFE OF FEAR.

God is love. When we take up permanent residence in a life of love, we live in God and God lives in us. This way, love has the run of the house, becomes at home and mature in us, so that we're free of worry on Judgment Day—our standing in the world is identical with Christ's. There is no room in love for fear. Well-formed love banishes fear. Since fear is crippling, a fearful life—fear of death, fear of judgment—is one not yet fully formed in love.

1 JOHN 4:17 MSG

God is for me, not against me. He is my Abba (Daddy) Father. He loves me with an everlasting, perfect love and holds me with his strong arms. Since God did not intend for me to live a fear-based life, I am free to live a life of love instead.

Fear comes in all shapes and sizes. It will overtake our lives if we let it. But it is not from God.

For God has not given us a spirit of fear and timidity, but of power, love, and self-discipline.

2 TIMOTHY 1:7

Don't be afraid, for I am with you. Don't be discouraged, for I am your God. I will strengthen you and help you. I will hold you up with my victorious right hand.

ISAIAH 41:10

- Would others describe you as a fearful person? Why or why not?
- What are some practical ways we can exercise more faith and less fear in our daily lives?

May you live a life full of faith, instead of a life full of fear.

There is no fear in love.

1 JOHN 4:18 KJV

Overcommitting.

Are you tired? Worn out? Burned out on religion? Come to me. Get away with me and you'll recover your life. I'll show you how to take a real rest. Walk with me and work with me—watch how I do it. Learn the unforced rhythms of grace. I won't lay anything heavy or ill-fitting on you. Keep company with me and you'll learn to live freely and lightly.

MATTHEW 11:28 MSG

Think about all that you've already done this month—all the people you've interacted with and all the appointments you made and kept. Then take note of some key phrases in the passage above and think about how they do (or don't) currently apply to your life right now:

Recover your life...

Take a real rest...

Learn the unforced rhythms of grace...

Live freely and lightly...

I don't know about you, but I hate to let people down. I found myself doing it today. A friend wanted to meet for lunch, and I should've said there was too much going

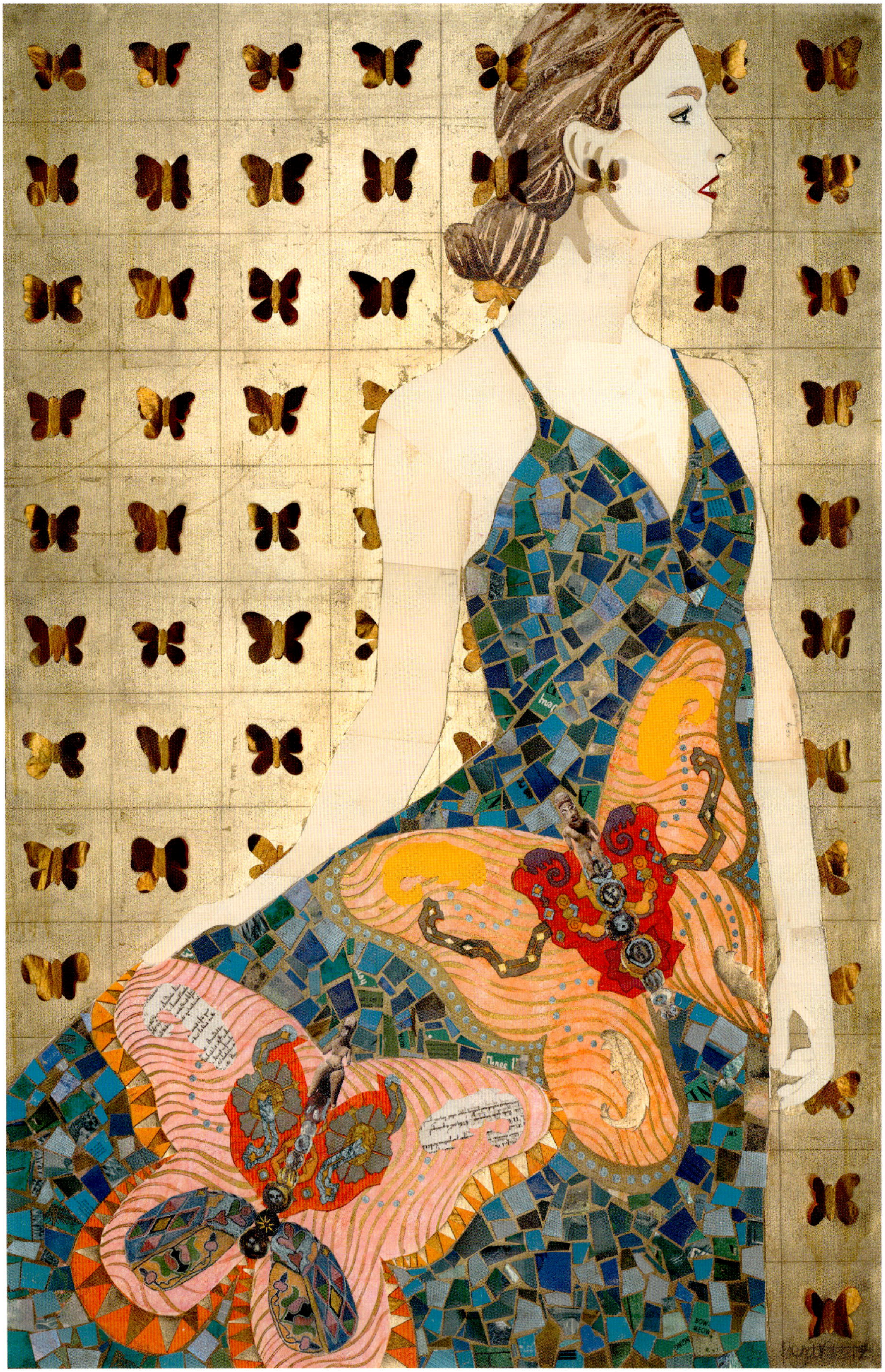

GRACE (LADIES IN GOLD)

on. Instead, I stressed myself out trying to juggle three other appointments. I work myself into these predicaments because I sometimes have a hard time saying "no."

I will never make everyone happy. When I say yes to something (or someone), I am always saying no to something (or someone) else. Think how our lives would be different if we lived more by the "unforced rhythms of grace" and less by our margin-less calendars.

> *For we are God's masterpiece. He has created us anew in Christ Jesus, so we can do the good things he planned for us long ago.*
>
> **EPHESIANS 2:10**

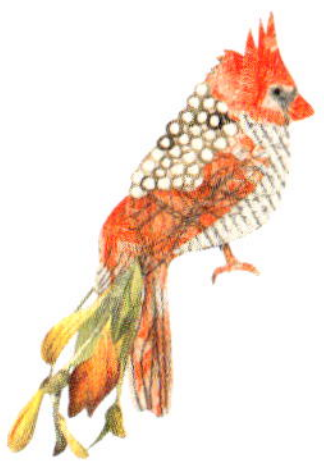

- What do you admire about someone who lives the "unforced rhythms of grace"?
- What could you change about your life in order to embrace one or more of these phrases?

May God fill you with a deep breath of assurance, knowing he can help you take the right path this week.

Just say a simple, "Yes, I will," or "No, I won't."

MATTHEW 5:37

Comparing.

For am I now seeking the approval of man, or of God? Or am I trying to please man? If I were still trying to please man, I would not be a servant of Christ.

GALATIANS 1:10 ESV

I remind myself often that I live before an audience of One. God's opinion of me is the only one that matters.

Constantly comparing myself to others = an unhappy life. There will always be someone with more money, more talent, more energy, and more stuff than me. Making a habit out of comparing our lives with others—noting what we do and don't have—often leads to depression and despair. We can't live up to what we think we're supposed to be or do. And we miss out on being and doing what God has planned just for us. I like how the British playwright, Oscar Wilde, put it: "Be yourself; everyone else is taken!"

Whenever you're all caught up in comparing yourself to others, remember that God is a safe place to land.

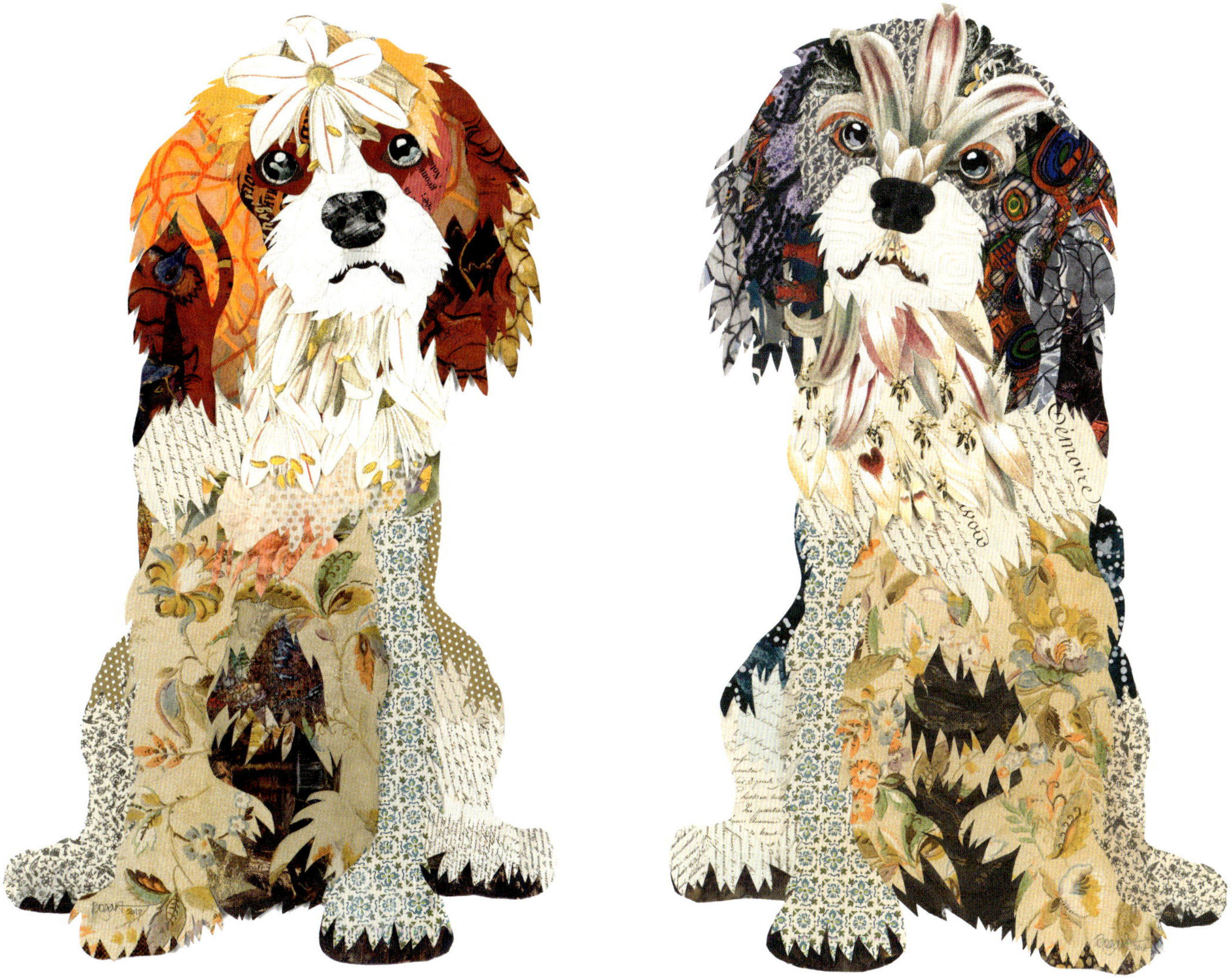

CAVALIER KING CHARLES DOGS

A peaceful heart leads to a healthy body;
jealousy is like cancer in the bones.

PROVERBS 14:30

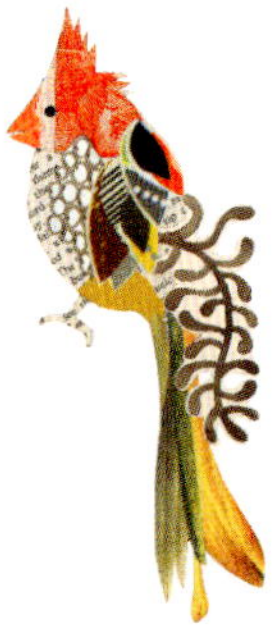

- When are you most likely to compare yourself with others?
- How can comparing lead to discontentment?

May God remind you today that you have everything you need.

Even strong young lions sometimes go hungry, but those who trust in the Lord will lack no good thing.

PSALM 34:10

FEAR OF CHANGE.

"For I know the plans I have for you," declares the Lord. "They are plans for good and not for disaster, to give you a future and a hope. In those days when you pray, I will listen. If you look for me wholeheartedly, you will find me. I will be found by you," says the Lord.

JEREMIAH 29:11-14

Change is certain. It's not *if* things will change but *how* they will change. How will we react to the changes around us?

Change happens to everyone. God is the only unchangeable, immutable being. The whole world had to stop for Covid-19. When I reflect on all that happened during that time, the highs and tragic lows, I realize I have much to be thankful for. I learned so much, and it changed my perspective on many issues that really matter. The change was hard, but it was also good.

If you are facing frightening changes right now, meditate on these verses. And ask yourself some questions (I'll get you started with some ideas).

What do these verses say about God and who he is?
(He has a plan for you!)

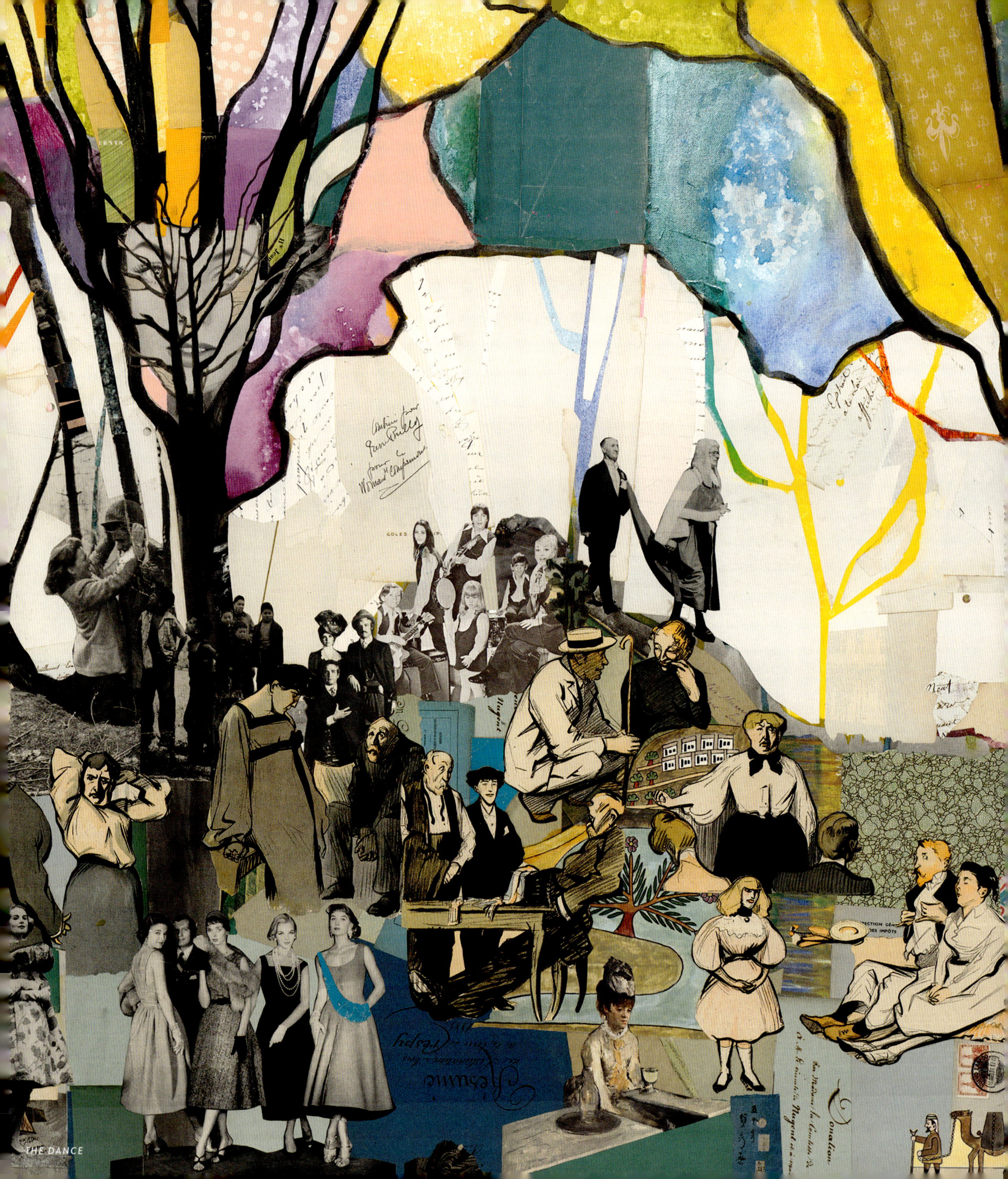

THE DANCE

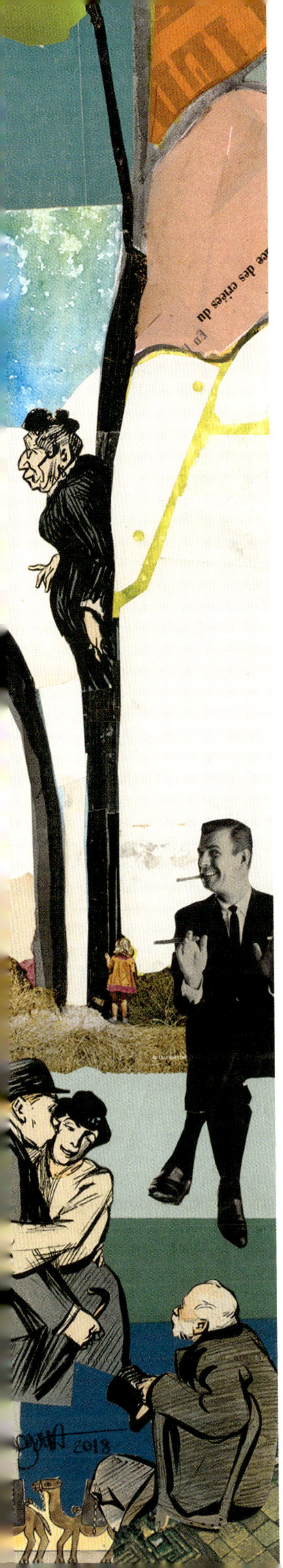

What is the commandment to obey? (Do not lose heart! Be strong and courageous! Do not be afraid or discouraged!)

What is the promise to cling to? (This affliction is momentary.)

I don't know what changes you are going through right now, but I do know this: God is still on his throne. Just remember, no matter what you are facing today, you will get through it with God by your side.

Jesus Christ is the same yesterday,
today and forever.

HEBREWS 13:8

So we do not lose heart. Though our outer
self is wasting away, our inner self is being
renewed day by day. For this light momentary
affliction is preparing for us an eternal
weight of glory beyond all comparison,
as we look not to the things that are seen
but to the things that are unseen. For the
things that are seen are transient, but
the things that are unseen are eternal.

2 CORINTHIANS 4:16-18 ESV

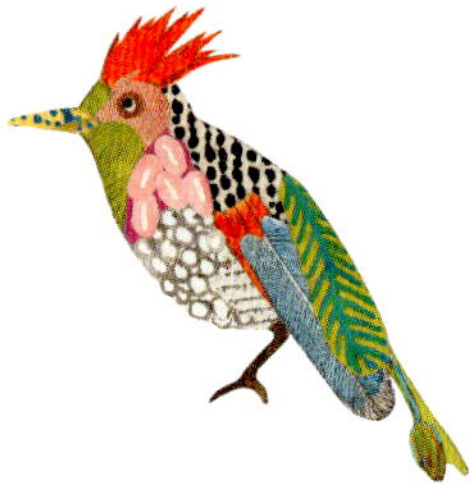

- How do you typically respond to change?
- How can prayer help you navigate life's greatest changes?

May God remind you of his steadfast presence when you need him most.

I am the Lord, and I do not change.

MALACHI 3:6

CHASING UNNECESSARY OBLIGATIONS.

Owe nothing to anyone—except for your obligation to love one another. If you love your neighbor, you will fulfill the requirements of God's law. For the commandments say, "You must not commit adultery. You must not murder. You must not steal. You must not covet." These—and other such commandments—are summed up in this one commandment: "Love your neighbor as yourself." Love does no wrong to others, so love fulfills the requirements of God's law.

ROMANS 13:8-10

I was talking to a friend recently about this very thing. She wisely reminded me to pray over my schedule daily and ask the Lord, "What do you have for me today?" She also reminded me that the Lord's burden is light and that I should not burden myself with things that are not mine to do. I'm trying to ask him to direct me throughout the day and to motivate me with love and joy to do only those things he has asked me to do—today.

When do you feel like unnecessary obligations are weighing heavily on you? What seemingly "urgent" thing or person demands your attention most often?

It bears repeating—when we say "no" to unnecessary obligations, we are saying "yes" to something greater. Many times throughout my day, I have to stop and ask myself, "Brenda, what goal are you chasing?"

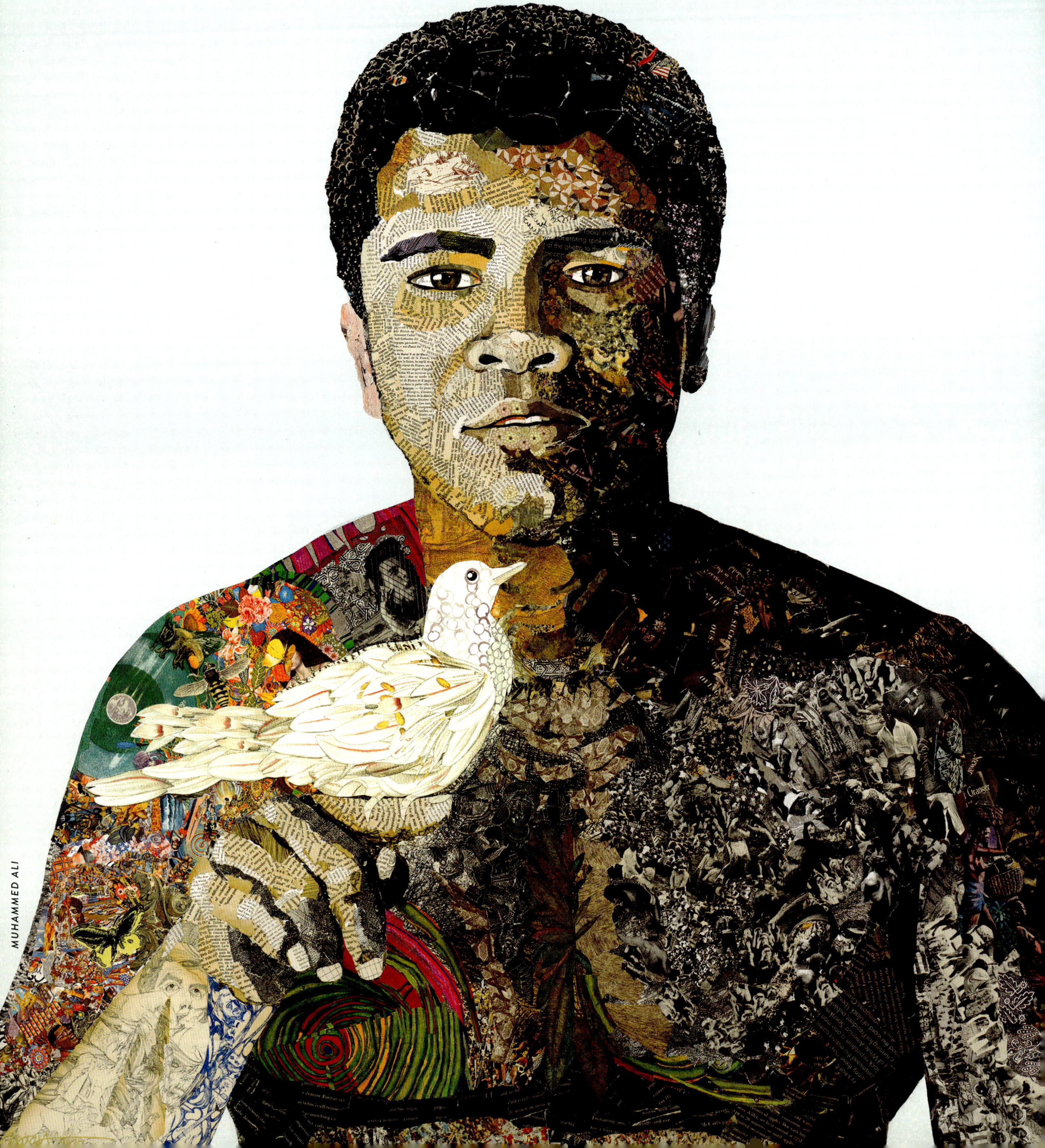

MUHAMMED ALI

I know it takes courage to say "no." It's a fight—and we must stay in the ring, intensely focused and undistracted.

Look carefully then how you walk, not as unwise but as wise, making the best use of the time, because the days are evil.

EPHESIANS 5:15-16 ESV

Yet God has made everything beautiful for its own time.

ECCLESIASTES 3:11

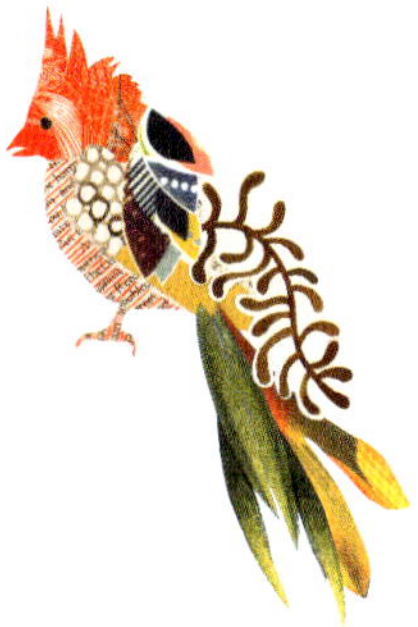

- What is difficult about managing our time each day?
- What are examples of unnecessary obligations?

Open your eyes to see what God has for you today.

So teach us to number our days that we may get a heart of wisdom.

PSALM 90:12 ESV

Self-Rejection.

O Lord, you have examined my heart and know everything about me. You know when I sit down or stand up. You know my thoughts even when I'm far away. You go before me and follow me. You place your hand of blessing on my head. You made all the delicate, inner parts of my body and knit me together in my mother's womb. Thank you for making me so wonderfully complex! Your workmanship is marvelous—how well I know it. You watched me as I was being formed in utter seclusion, as I was woven together in the dark of the womb. You saw me before I was born. Every day of my life was recorded in your book. Every moment was laid out before a single day had passed. How precious are your thoughts about me, O God. They cannot be numbered!

PSALM 139:1-2,5; 13-14,17

Did you know there is no one who has ever lived, or will live, who is exactly like you? You are uniquely and wonderfully made. No one can do what you do, the way you do it.

And yet, we are so easily tempted to fall into the trap of self-rejection, pointing out what we do not like about ourselves and wondering why God made us this way. But

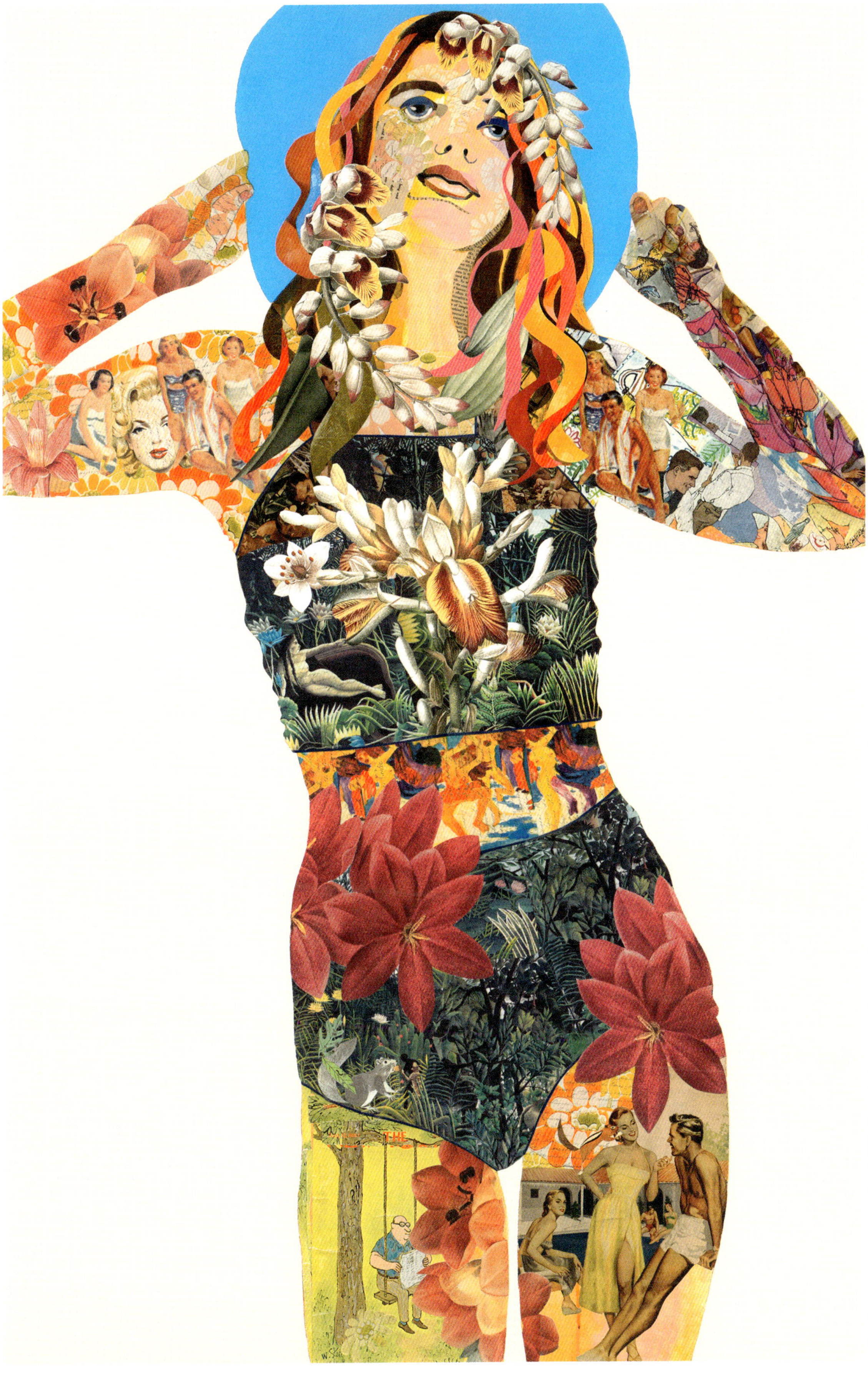

BIKINI GIRL (JUNGLE G RL)

when I look at nature, I see God designed animals and flowers for their specific and unique purpose in life. In the same way, I am reminded that he created me and my personality, talents, and gifts to accomplish a certain purpose that no one else can do. There is no one else like you, and God created you to do things in a way that no one else can duplicate. I love thinking about that. Especially when I feel defeated or that I'm not accomplishing anything.

Look closely at the details of your personality, your life experiences, your gifts—all the things that make you unique from every other human being on earth. There is much more to you than meets the eye. Our sovereign God loves *you* beyond all measure just the way you are.

> *Thank you for making me so wonderfully complex! Your workmanship is marvelous—how well I know it.*
>
> **PSALM 139:14-16**

> *So now there is no condemnation for those who belong to Christ Jesus.*
>
> **ROMANS 8:1**

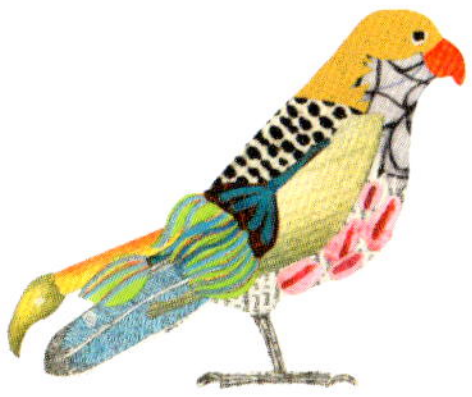

- When are you most likely to fall into a trap of self-rejection?
- What is unique about how God made you?

May God bless you with eyes to see your real beauty.

You are altogether beautiful, my love; there is no flaw in you...

SONG OF SOLOMON 4:7 ESV

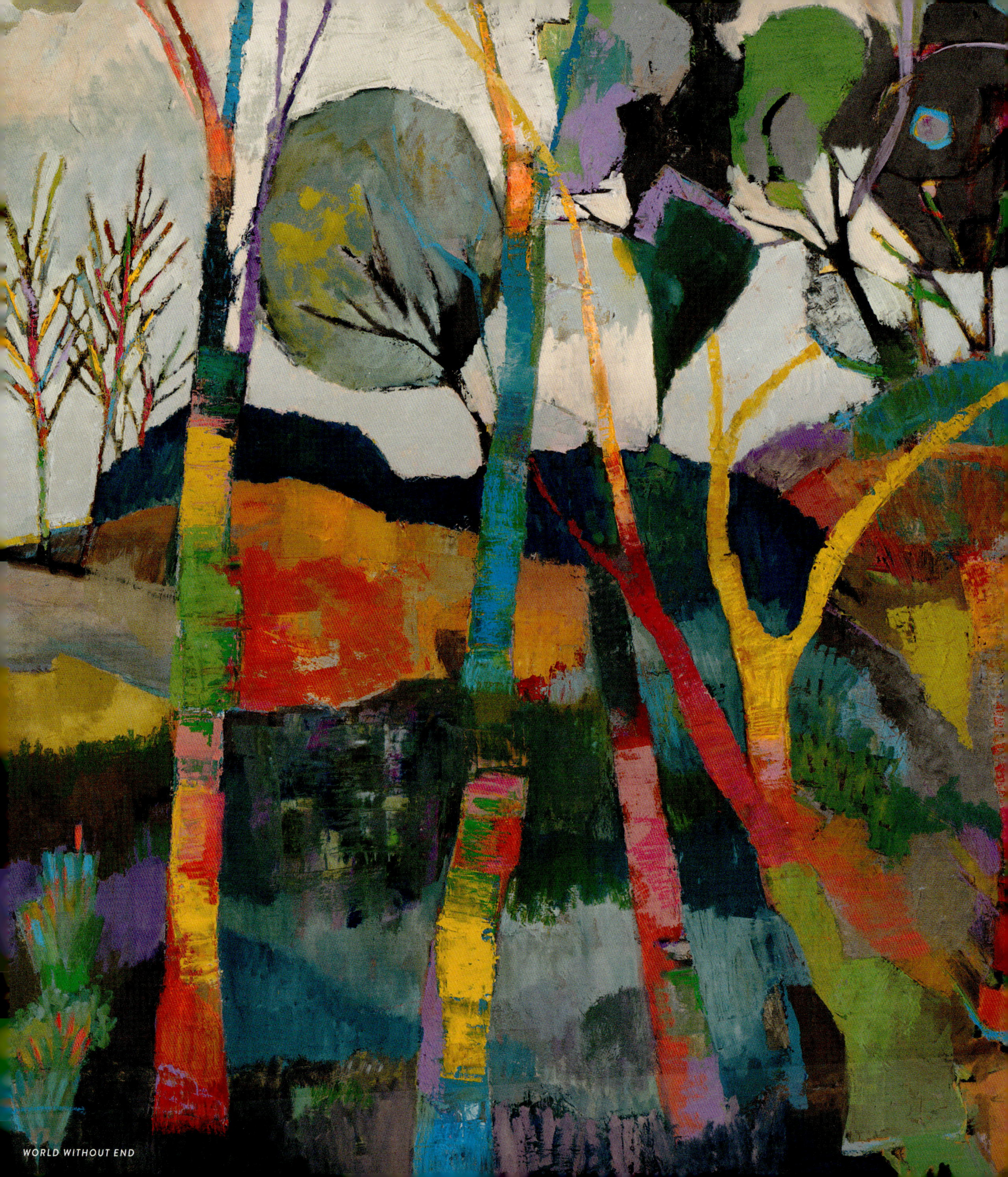

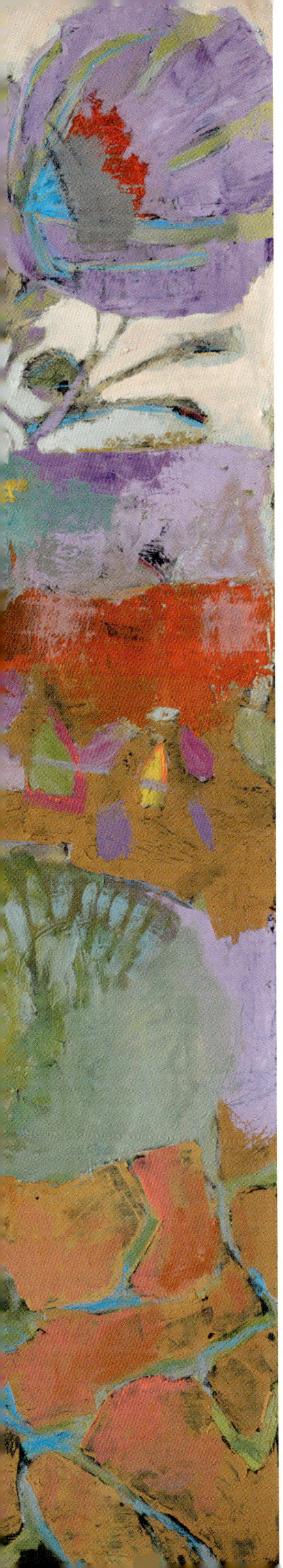

Ignoring the Sabbath Rest.

> *So the creation of the heavens and the earth and everything in them was completed. On the seventh day God had finished his work of creation, so he rested from all his work. And God blessed the seventh day and declared it holy, because it was the day when he rested from all his work of creation.*
>
> **GENESIS 2:1-3**

What does a Sabbath rest look like to you?

If you're like me, you like to take a nap on Sundays. But is that all God means by taking a "Sabbath rest" one day a week? I'm learning that it is a whole lot more than just taking a nap!

On the Sabbath, God invites us to taste a bit of heaven. He calls us to "drink in the best of me on this day." To find our true rest in him. Like the taking in of the bread and wine, he invites us to taste a piece of our future life with him in eternity.

The Sabbath is a day to soak in God's Word, worship him, rest from a normal day's work, and to dip our big toe into the "real" world without end. The world where there is no sorrow or suffering because the flame of God's glory is so bright it will burn off all that isn't holy and good. This is our permanent future home. A real place that has been promised to us by our Creator.

So enjoy this day for the gift that it is!

And he said to them, "The Sabbath was made for man, not man for the Sabbath."

MARK 2:27 ESV

Seek the Lord while you can find him. Call on him now while he is near.

ISAIAH 55:6

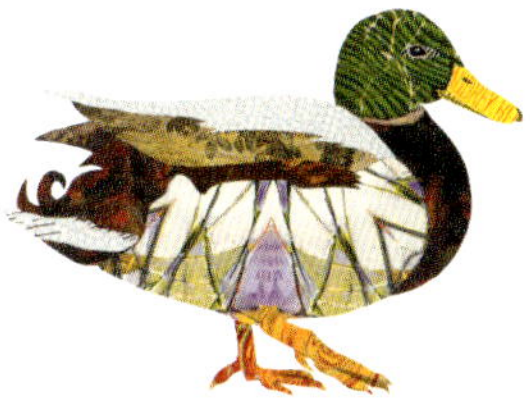

- Why do you think God said one day should be different, set apart from the other days of the week?
- What can we do (or stop doing) to be more refreshed spiritually and physically on this day?

May God grant you his rest this week.

The Lord replied, "...I will give you rest—everything will be fine for you."

EXODUS 33:14

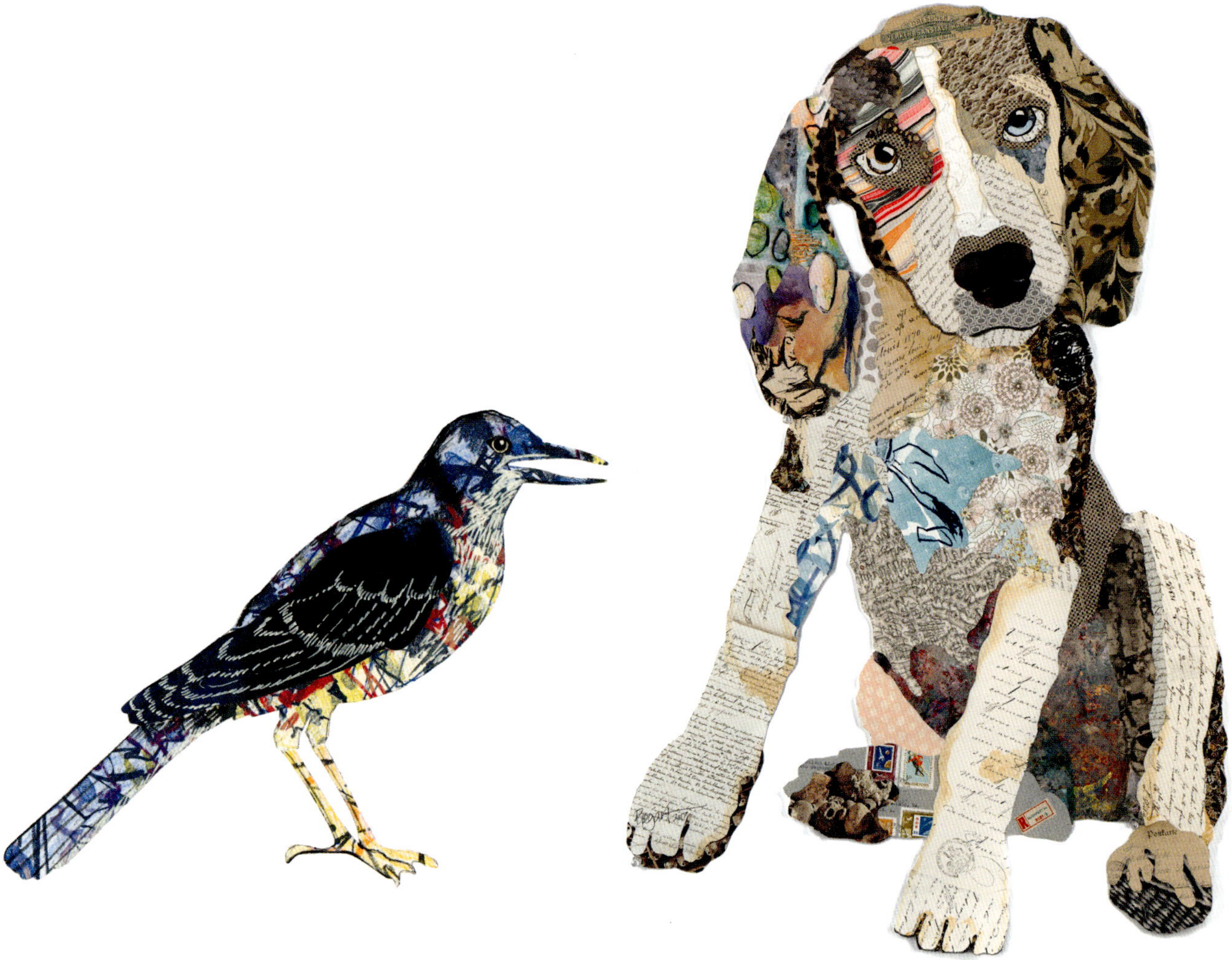

MOCKINGBIRD 69, BEAGLE

GIVING UNSOLICITED ADVICE.

Understand this, my dear brothers and sisters: You must all be quick to listen, slow to speak, and slow to get angry.

JAMES 1:19

A wise friend recently commented, "Giving unsolicited advice is often received as criticism." As a mother of adult children, this one is so hard. And it's not just my adult children who are subject to my generous doses of unsolicited advice. It seems everyone in my path is a potential victim. Thank you, wise friend, for helping me be more self-aware!

The best antidote to giving unsolicited advice is to listen *more* and talk *less.* Are you "quick" to listen, like the Bible says in James? Or are you interrupting with your reply, instead of listening to the heart behind someone's words?

Spouting off before listening to the facts is both shameful and foolish.

PROVERBS 18:13

Fools have no interest in understanding; they only want to air their own opinions.

PROVERBS 18:2

Even fools are thought wise when they keep silent;
with their mouths shut, they seem intelligent.

PROVERBS 17:28

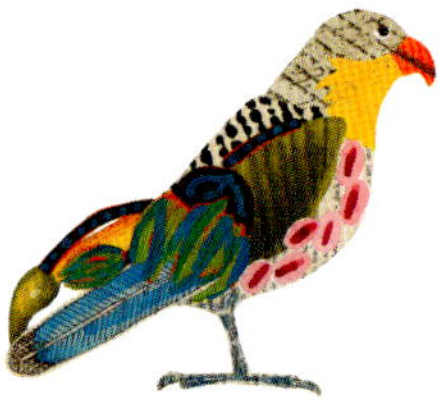

- Why do you think unsolicited advice might often come across as criticism?
- How does it feel when someone gives you advice that you did not seek?

May God hold our tongues for us—and open our ears.

Watch your tongue and keep your mouth shut,
and you will stay out of trouble.

PROVERBS 21:23

Unnecessary Drama.

A soft answer turns away wrath, but a harsh word stirs up anger.

PROVERBS 15:1 ESV

We have more power in our words than we probably realize. The ability of a soft answer to turn away another person's wrath is not to be underestimated. But it takes strength and restraint. The Bible is clear. We're told not to get sucked into foolish arguments that tear apart delicate relationships.

Endlessly rehearsing who did what in a relationship gets nowhere. It is unnecessary drama that accomplishes only further distraction, destruction, and despair. Our only hope is to remain focused on our vertical spiritual relationship (between us and God) to keep us from creating drama in our horizontal, earthly relationships with others. If only we can stay focused on him, it will help all our relationships.

Again I say, don't get involved in foolish, ignorant arguments that only start fights. A servant of the Lord must not quarrel but must be kind to everyone, be able to teach, and be patient with difficult people.

2 TIMOTHY 2:23-24

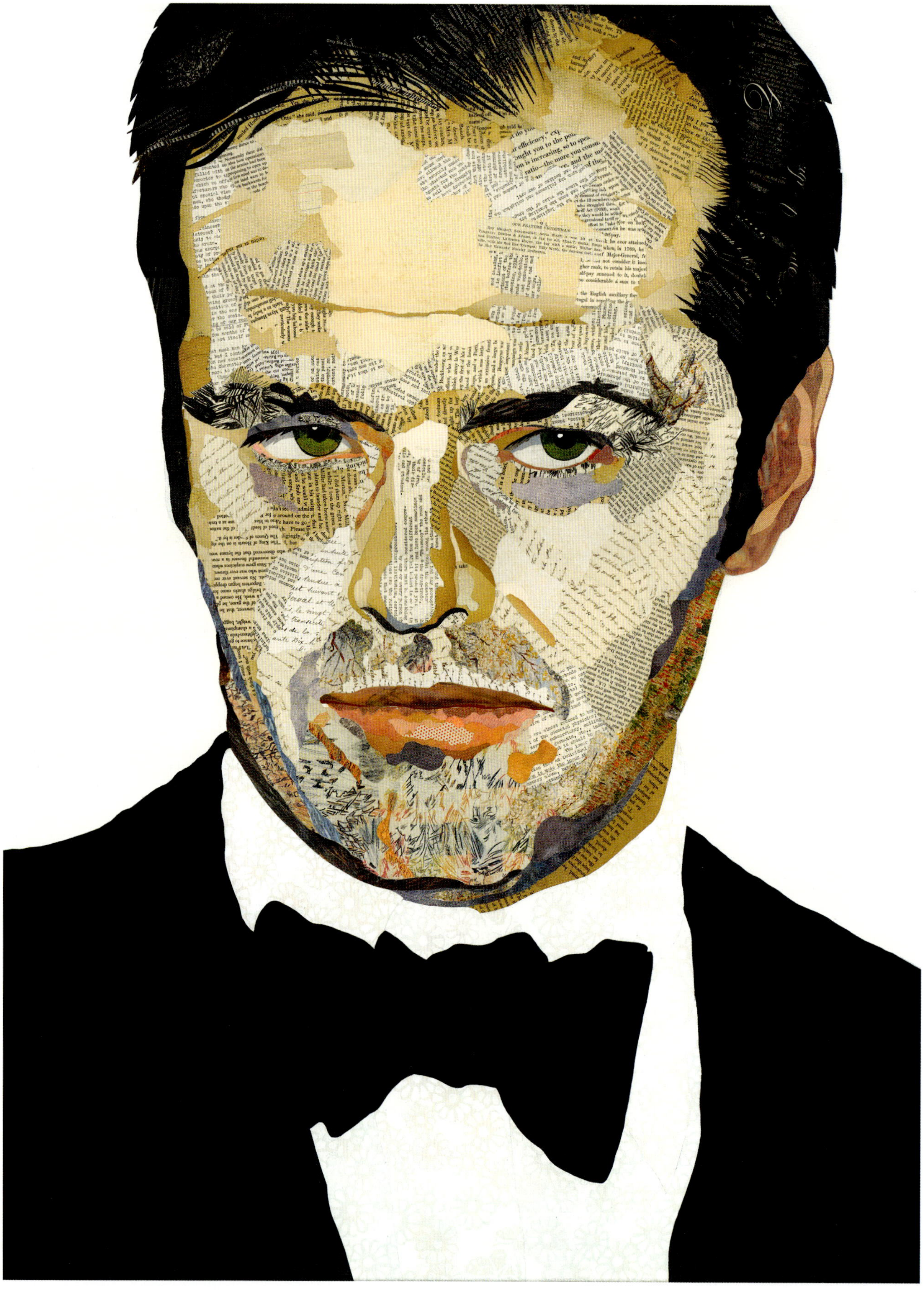

JACK NICHOLSON

But if you are always biting and devouring one another, watch out! Beware of destroying one another. So I say, let the Holy Spirit guide your lives. Then you won't be doing what your sinful nature craves.

GALATIANS 5:15-16

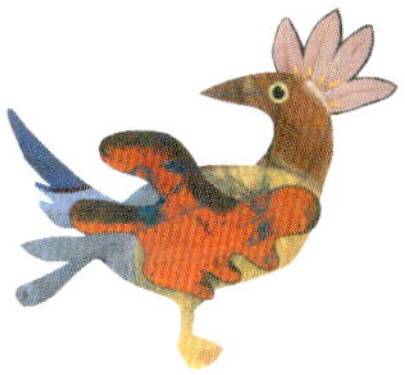

- How do arguments and gossip create unnecessary drama?
- What are some ways to reduce the unnecessary drama in your life?

May God give you greater wisdom with your words.

Blessed are the peacemakers...

MATTHEW 5:9 KJV

LISTENING TO ARGUE.

Instead, we will speak the truth in love, growing in every way more and more like Christ, who is the head of his body, the church.

EPHESIANS 4:15

Listening to argue says, "My opinion is right. Yours is wrong." That attitude tears down relationships. Listening to *understand,* on the other hand, shows respect and love and is relationship-building. I do not have to agree; I just listen with genuine interest, repeating back what I heard the other person say to make sure I correctly understood their point. When I've accurately repeated back to someone what they are saying, they know they were listened to. And with truth and love I can then genuinely say, "I'm not there with you yet, but I want to thank you for taking the time to explain this to me. I more fully understand your thoughts, beliefs, and opinion."

Learning and applying this communication skill changed my life.

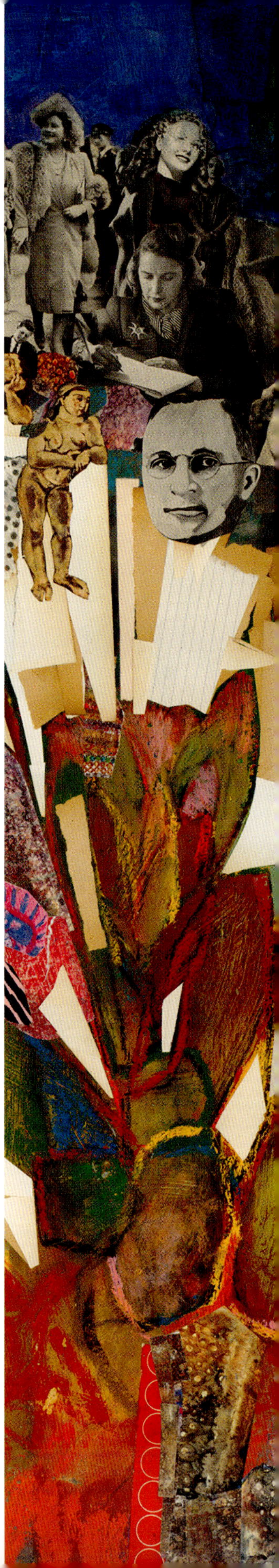

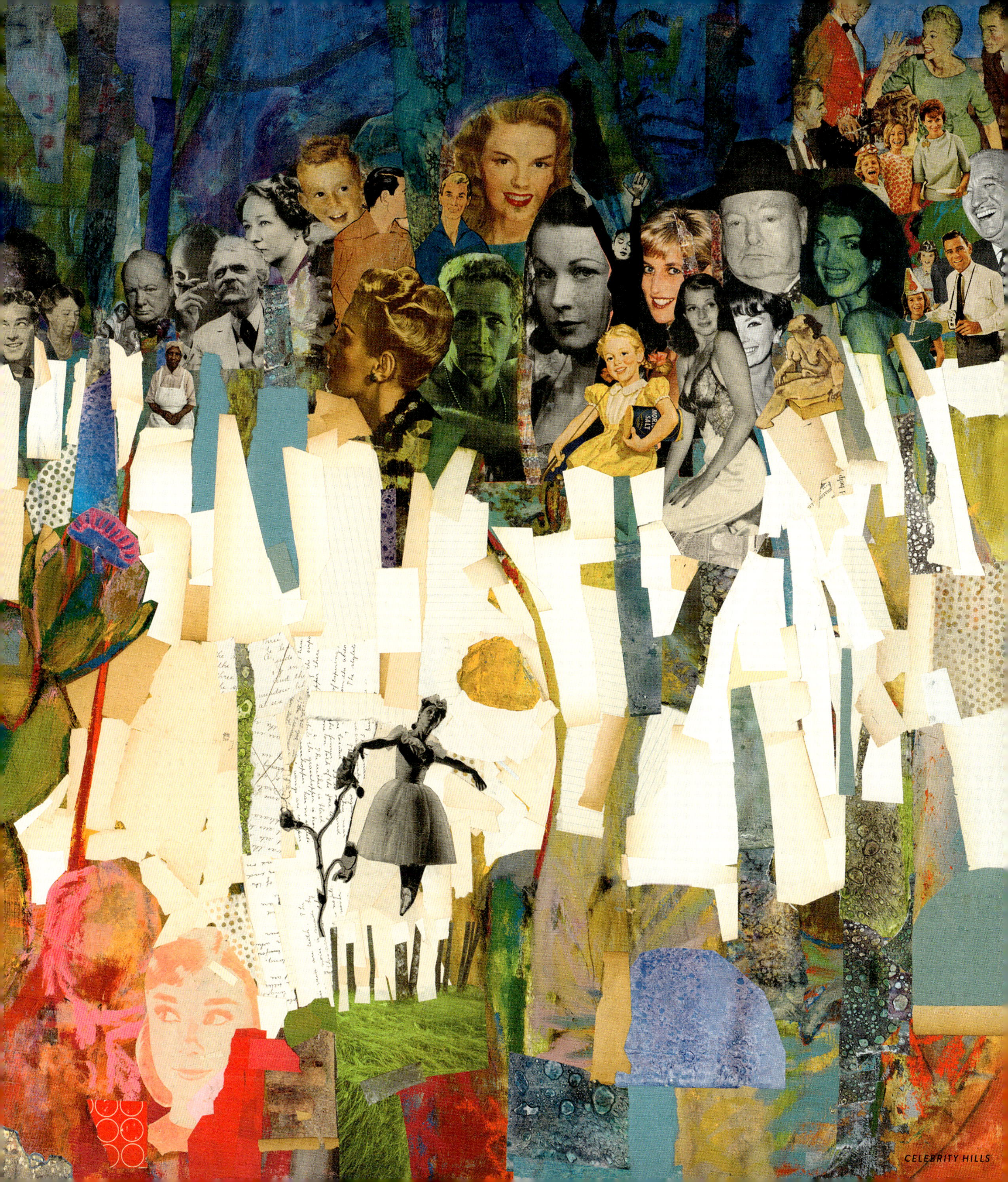

CELEBRITY HILLS

I no longer had to defend my opinion. Or argue my side. I could stop thinking about formulating my rebuttal and, instead, intently listen to the other person. Learning this principle made all my relationships better and more at peace...even if we disagreed strongly about an issue.

Listening to understand is an important part of good communication. This is especially true in marriage. Our spouse is not the enemy—we are on the same team. So if God's goal for marriage is that we live out the gospel to each other and to the world, why wouldn't I be a safe harbor for my husband? The steady place to land. It's home, really. I want to be the place he craves, the desire of his heart. Loving him well means I am not going to react to every offense. I am not going to take everything personally. I am not going to react to his bad mood or slight offense, as if it has something to do with me. Instead, I am going to be a safe place for him to unfurl from the world, a place to emote about all the hurts in his heart, an ear and heart that listen well without trying to fix it.

They must not slander anyone and must avoid quarreling. Instead, they should be gentle and show true humility to everyone.

TITUS 3:2

Never pay back evil with more evil. Do things in such a way that everyone can see you are honorable.

ROMANS 12:17

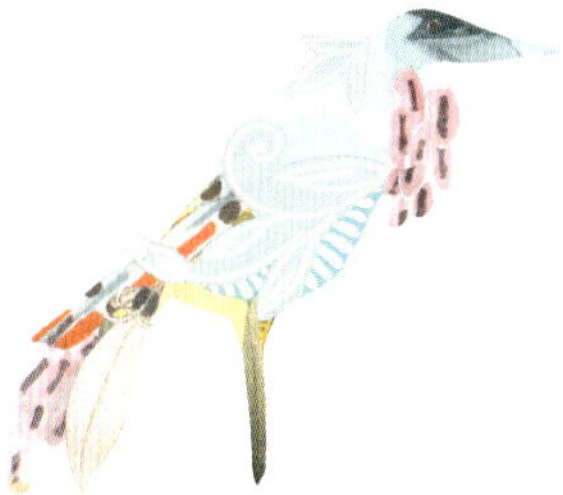

- Are you a good listener? Why or why not?
- Try applying this skill in the next week or so. Then reflect. How did it help your conversation and build your relationship?

May God open your ears and your heart to others.

Love each other with genuine affection...

ROMANS 12:10

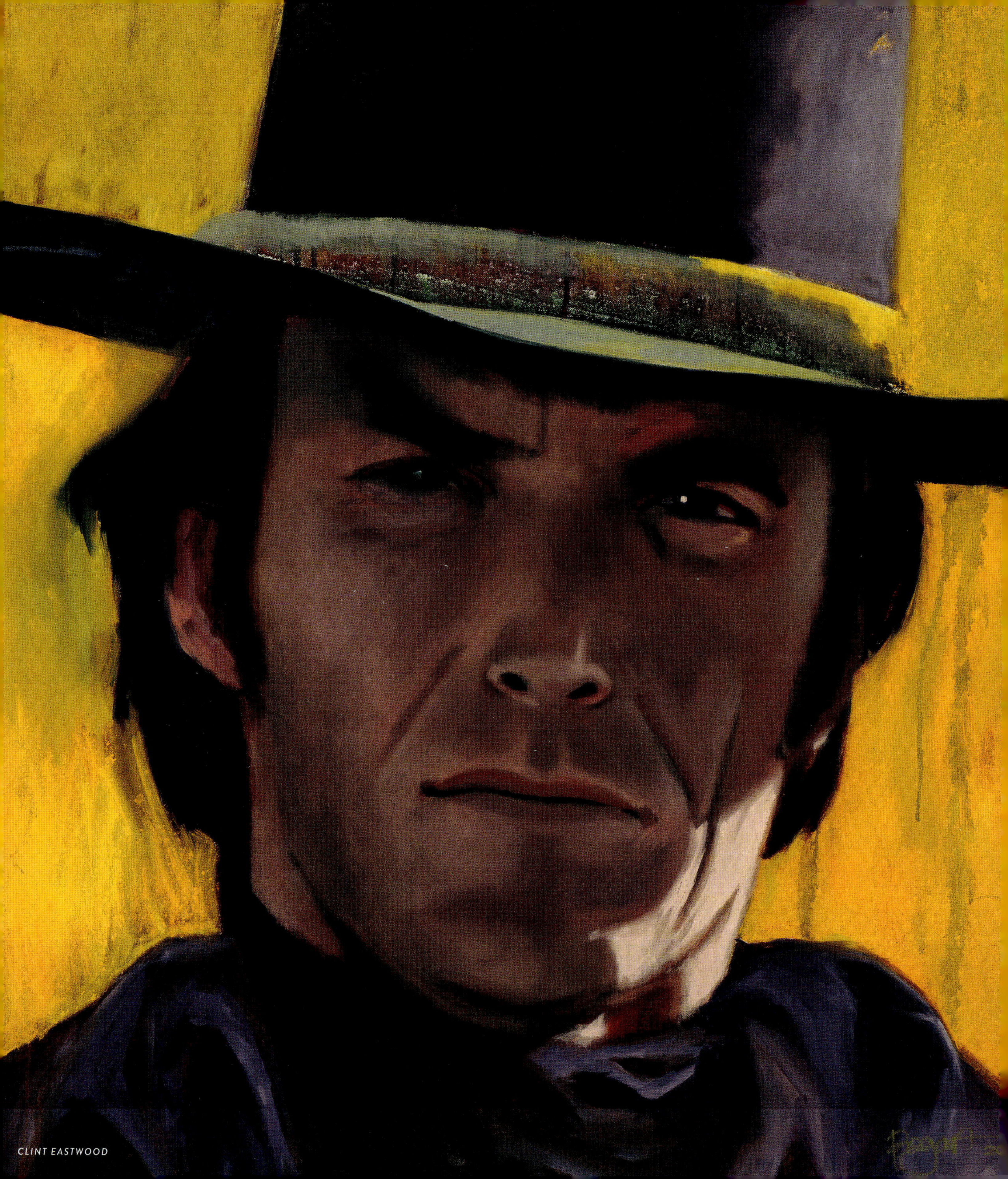

CLINT EASTWOOD

Fear of the Unknown.

But now, O Jacob, listen to the Lord who created you. O Israel, the one who formed you says, "Do not be afraid, for I have ransomed you. I have called you by name; you are mine. When you go through deep waters, I will be with you. When you go through rivers of difficulty, you will not drown. When you walk through the fire of oppression, you will not be burned up; the flames will not consume you."

ISAIAH 43:1-2

I know what it's like to fear the unknown. Years ago I went through a life-altering, agonizing experience. At times, it brought out the worst in me in ways I deeply regret. I was fearful because I had no idea how the situation was going to resolve.

The fear of the unknown is devastating. Questions flood our minds about things over which we have no control. *What will happen now? Will my life ever be normal again?*

During this painful season where so much was uncertain, I clung to this verse in Isaiah to remind me of what I *did know* to be true. I plastered this verse all over my home, in my handbag, on my bathroom mirror, and even in my car!

Whenever I saw these words, several things happened.

They reminded me of many of God's promises.

They helped me to remember that I am indeed God's child.

They helped me to trust that it is impossible for him to let go of me.

They helped ease my fear of the unknown.

Whenever I am going through difficulty, God promises to navigate the deep waters for me. When I reflect on that experience from my past, I remember the pain. But I also recall God's loving tenderness to me when I needed it most. The journey was heart-wrenching. But it was also good. Honestly, I am now thankful for that time simply because of all it taught me—and how God grew me through it.

> *See, God has come to save me. I will trust in him and not be afraid.*
> *The Lord God is my strength and my song; he has given me victory.*
>
> **ISAIAH 12:2**

> *Trust in the Lord with all your heart; do not depend on your own understanding. Seek his will in all you do, and he will show you which path to take.*
>
> **PROVERBS 3:5-6**

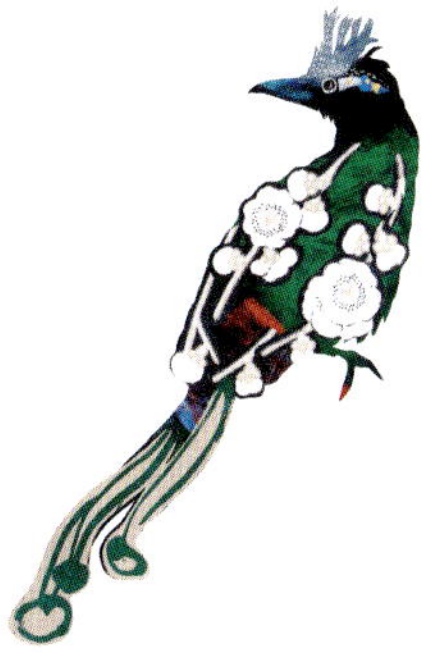

- When was a time you really dreaded the future? Why?
- What can we do whenever we are tempted to be afraid of the unknown?

Take a deep breath. May God remind you throughout the day, "Trust me."

But if we look forward to something we don't yet have, we must wait patiently and confidently.

ROMANS 8:25

Forgetting Children Are Our Guests.

I have no greater joy than to hear that my children are walking in the truth.

3 JOHN 1:4 ESV

I still miss it. The after-school chaos of kids busting through the door and sliding their backpacks across the kitchen table. The neighborhood kids walking up the street with their project posters rolled under their arms, wanting my help.

We spend all these years nurturing and meeting our children's every need, then just like that, it's over. They move away, marry a stranger, and your world is suddenly much quieter. But that's also when you know you got some things right! You helped shape and mold an independent, self-sufficient human who is contributing to the well-being of the world. It's a sweet hurt.

Still, I see more parents clinging to their adult children in unhealthy ways. They refuse to let go of their authority and guilt their children into all sorts of things that only cause division and resentment. When I see the pain of the kids, I know I do it too.

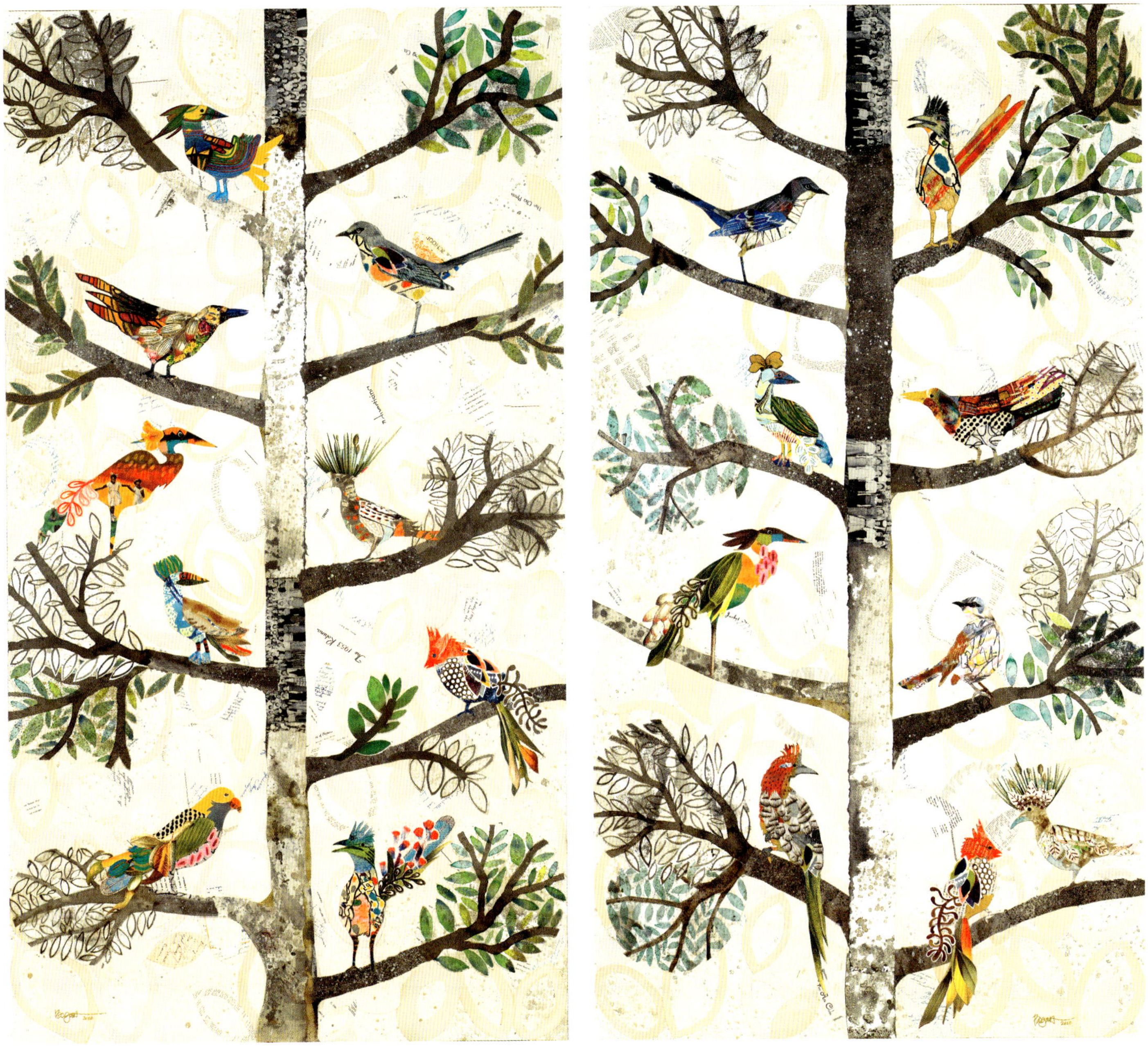

TREE OF LIFE 1, 2

My husband and I are involved in marriage ministry. Do you know the number one stress we encounter with newly married couples? Dominating parents. I have learned a lot from these young couples. Transitions are tough. Things are rarely in a straight line, and we're not parents very long before realizing we are never going to do this perfectly. Learning to let go and trust children to make their own mistakes—and seeing them form a new family unit and make their spouse their primary earthly concern—well, it's a sweet joy! Then there's the day when our adult child says something so wise (that they learned from us as a child but we were certain they never heard). And the best part is that they think it's their idea! If that day hasn't already happened, I hope it will. It's the best feeling!

Do to others whatever you would like them to do to you. This is the essence of all that is taught in the law and the prophets.

MATTHEW 7:12

Children are a gift from the Lord; they are a reward from him.

PSALM 127:3

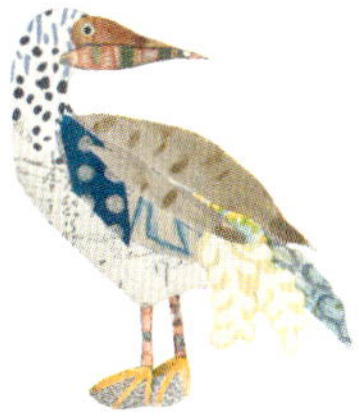

- How do you see parents holding too tightly to their adult children?
- What is the best parenting advice you've ever heard?

May God direct your family—now and in the future.

I will teach all your children, and they will enjoy great peace.

ISAIAH 54:13

COMPLAINING.

Then I realized that my heart was bitter, and I was all torn up inside. I was so foolish and ignorant—I must have seemed like a senseless animal to you. Yet I still belong to you; you hold my right hand. You guide me with your counsel, leading me to a glorious destiny.

PSALM 73:21-24

Like swarming gnats is my complaining spirit. And often my complaints are against the very best things God has used to bless me—my family, my relationships, my work. I am sitting here disgusted with myself and crying as I write. How does this cycle happen? God blesses me, and then I complain about the blessing!

It's hard to be a portrait of beauty and grace in life when all we want to do is complain. That's not exactly what we want to be remembered for doing. Like Israel complaining about God's generous provision of manna, I need to remember God's faithfulness to provide all that I need, and yes, sometimes it is a wild ride through the desert. I have to remember that God is not harsh or scary. He is gentle and loving. And he wants to take us on an adventure! I'm just *so* easily distracted by my many complaints when I get off track and start living by "the world according to Brenda" instead of following God.

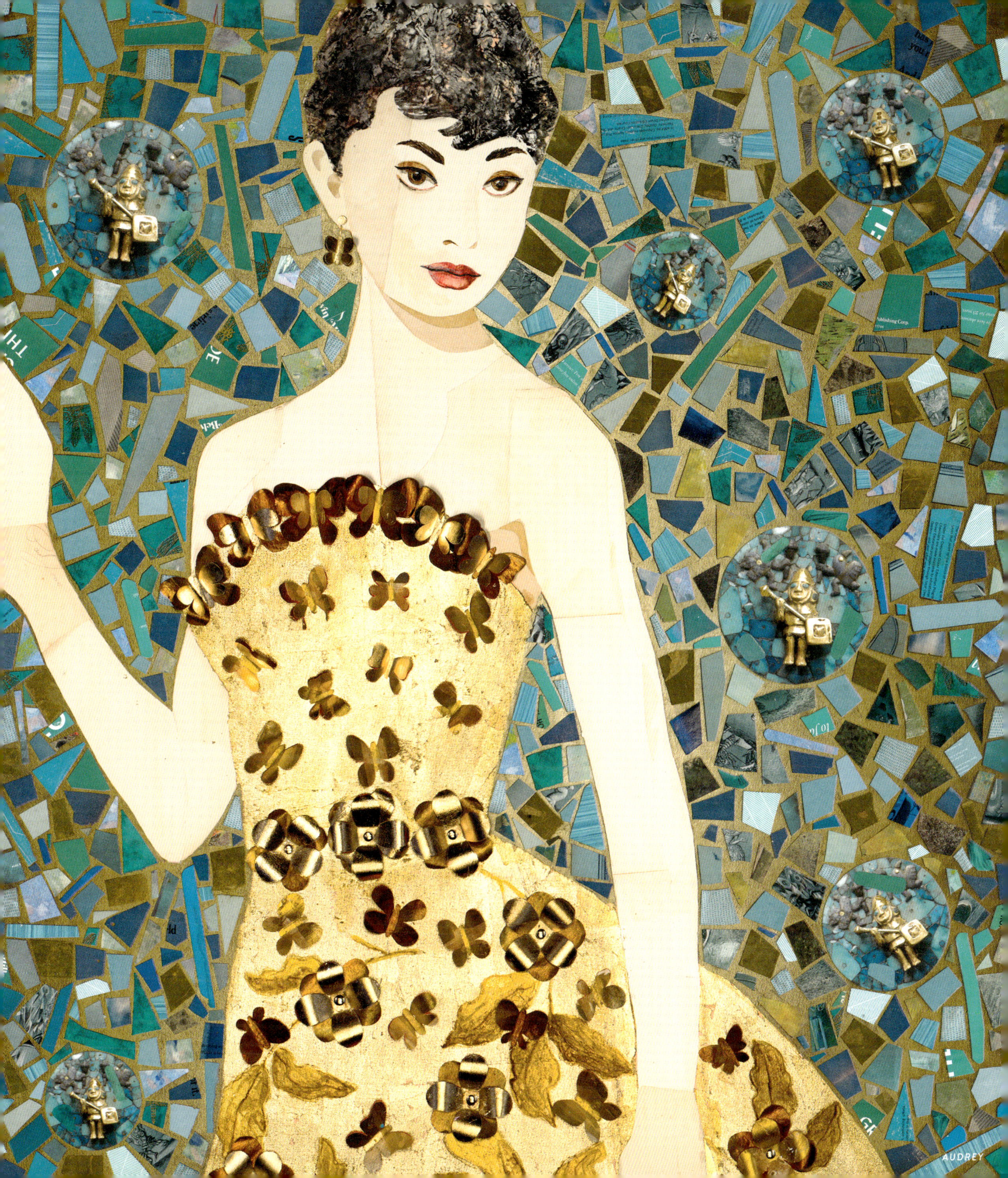
AUDREY

Be thankful in all circumstances, for this is God's will for you who belong to Christ Jesus.

1 THESSALONIANS 5:18

Then Moses said to Aaron, "Announce this to the entire community of Israel: 'Present yourselves before the Lord, for he has heard your complaining.'"

EXODUS 16:9

For more on this topic, read Philippians 2:12-16.

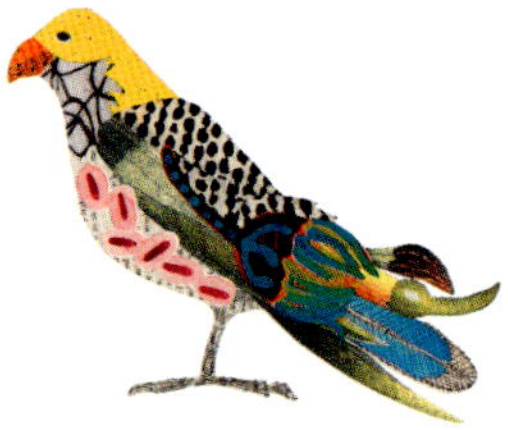

- What causes you to complain most often?
- Why are our complaints like "little gnats"?

May this be your mantra:
Praise more, Complain less.

"Do everything without complaining..."

PHILIPPIANS 2:14

Fear of Failure.

Therefore, since we are surrounded by such a great cloud of witnesses, let us throw off everything that hinders and the sin that so easily entangles. And let us run with perseverance the race marked out for us, fixing our eyes on Jesus, the author and perfecter of our faith.

HEBREWS 12:1-2 NIV

I often ask myself, "What could I accomplish if my desire to succeed was greater than my fear of failing?" For years, decades really, I was afraid to be who God made me to be. I didn't answer his call to run the race he set before me because I was afraid to fail and let others down. My true identity has increasingly been in the Lord who created me. God bent me a certain way, yet I have struggled most of my life to be that person (while at the same time pleasing those around me). That strategy really doesn't ever work. I didn't fully respect the call God had on my life. My fears trumped my desire to live freely as the person he made me to be.

It is not the responsibility of those around me to make sure I follow my calling. It has always been mine. And the slow drag to get there has been largely based on fear.

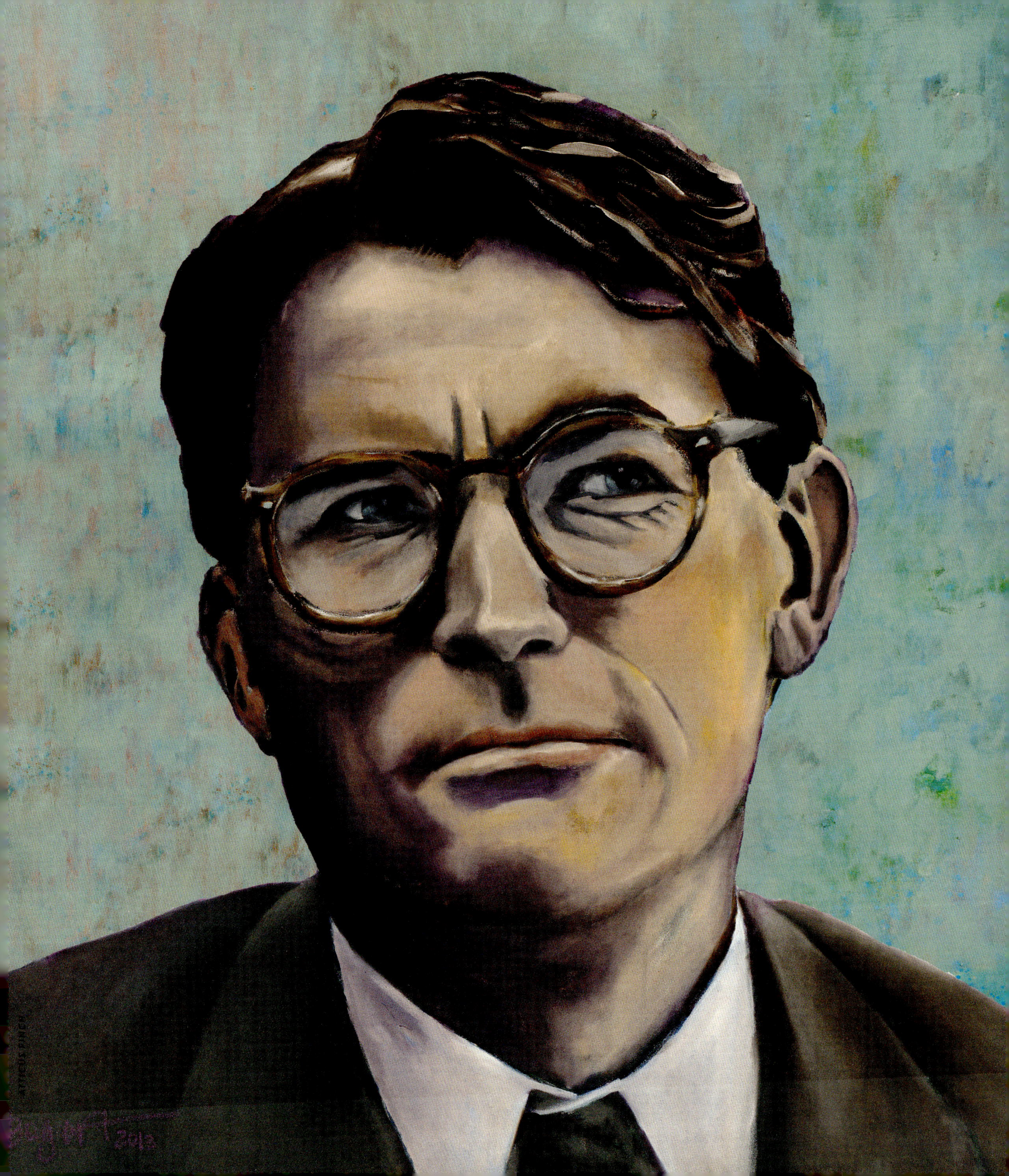

ATTICUS FINCH

Fear of disappointing the people in my life.

Fear of failing in the world's eyes.

And here's the real kicker—I even feared being so overcome by my calling that I would be completely overtaken by it, like an addict to her drug. I can laugh now, but that was a legitimate fear at one time! Like a trapped lion finally let out of her cage, I feared losing control over myself once I gave in and fully explored who God called me to be. No wonder there are so many classic books and storylines about having the *courage* to be who you are meant to be.

So I have to ask, "Are you afraid to be who God called *you* to be? Who—or what—are you blaming for your current situation?"

Be strong and courageous. Do not be afraid or terrified because of them, for the Lord your God goes with you; he will never leave you nor forsake you.

DEUTERONOMY 31:6

The Lord is with me; I will not be afraid.
What can mere mortals do to me?

PSALM 118:6 NIV

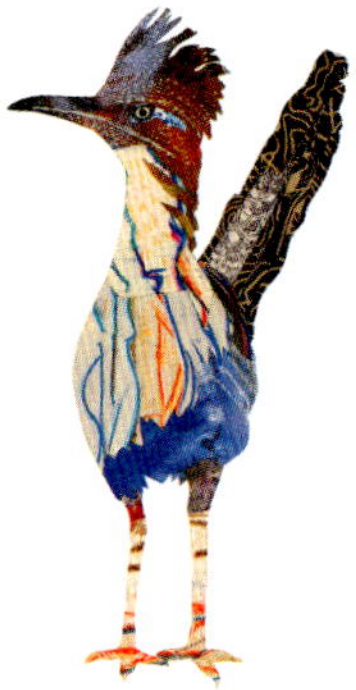

- Where do you place your primary identity?
- What are your greatest fears about failure?

May your desire to succeed overcome the fear of failure.

...though I fall, I will rise again.

MICAH 7:8

HOARDING TALENTS.

For it will be like a man going on a journey, who called his servants and entrusted to them his property. To one he gave five talents, to another two, to another one, to each according to his ability. Then he went away. He who had received the five talents went at once and traded with them, and he made five talents more. So also he who had the two talents made two talents more. But he who had received the one talent went and dug in the ground and hid his master's money.

MATTHEW 25:14-29

A "talent" in this parable refers to an amount of silver, a form of currency in Jesus' time. Today, we think about this parable in the sense that God gave each of us "talents" or gifts. For example, some have a God-given talent for encouraging or empathizing with others, while some are gifted at organizing people and things. To some, God also gives artistic talents, or the ability to create wealth, or business expertise...you get the idea.

God made you uniquely *you.* Did you know there is no one else in the universe exactly like you? No one can do what you do the *way* you do it. The bad guy in this parable is the one who did nothing with his talent. He just buried it. Fear is a form of pride that can keep us from using our gift. Sometimes we're afraid to use the gift,

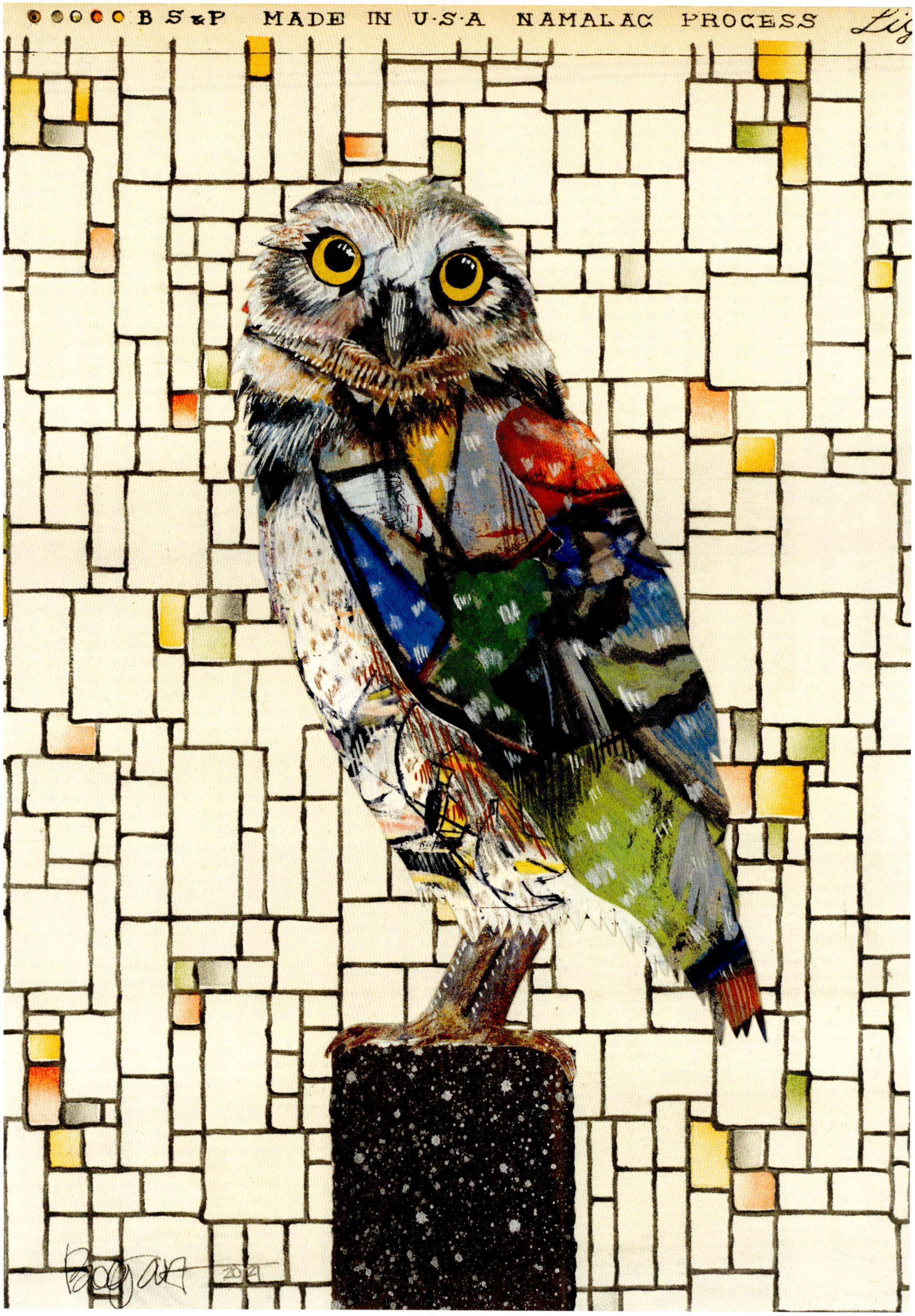

SCREECH OWL 2

even though we hear it calling to us from the very dirt in which we've buried it! Are we going to continue letting our pride get in the way of uncovering the gifts God gave us?

What are some new ways that we can use the gifts God has given us? Here's an idea. Start by asking him to show you what your gifts are. Pay attention to what activities give you energy. Once you know what your talents are, pray for God to show you *new* and unique ways he wants you to use your specific gifts. Then spend 5–10 minutes writing every crazy idea that comes into your head. Keep writing. Don't listen to the voices that tell you why your ideas won't work! Just let the ideas flow. I would love to hear what happens next.

> *You are the light of the world—like a city on a hilltop that cannot be hidden. No one lights a lamp and then puts it under a basket. Instead, a lamp is placed on a stand, where it gives light to everyone in the house.*
>
> **MATTHEW 5:14-15**

> *So, whether you eat or drink, or whatever you do, do all to the glory of God.*
>
> **1 CORINTHIANS 10:31 ESV**

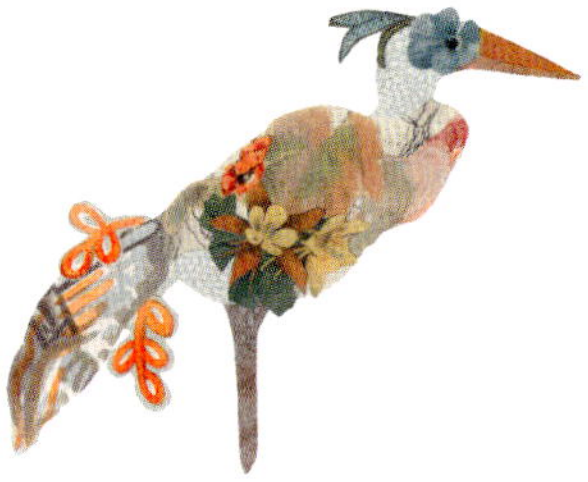

- What do you think are some of your God-given gifts?
- How are you using your gifts right now?

May God inspire you to dream **big** and try something **new**.

For God is working in you, giving you the desire and the power to do what pleases him.

PHILIPPIANS 2:13

The Right to Be Angry.

Get rid of all bitterness, rage, anger, harsh words, and slander, as well as all types of evil behavior. Instead, be kind to each other, tenderhearted, forgiving one another, just as God through Christ has forgiven you.

EPHESIANS 4:31-32

He said the package was hand-delivered to our door at 5:30, but we did not receive it. We asked the neighbors on both sides, but no package. It contained our personal information including social security numbers, as well as our health and financial information. We eventually discovered the wrong address was on the address label and the package was delivered directly across the street. They were out of town, but thankfully they had someone retrieve it for us.

I wanted to get angry, shame the person who made the mistake, and possibly sever that relationship (but just for a moment). So here is what God did to redeem the entire situation. This is the fascinating part of the story. We had been wanting to connect more with the couple across the street, and this package gave us a reason to invite them over. Three days later we sat together in our home. They were so excited to learn about my LOVE campaign for North Texas Food Bank and immediately bought and promoted the purchase of several prints, which translated into thousands of meals for North Texans. A friendship deepened and needy people were fed—all because of a connection made through a missing package.

Now back to the guy who got the address wrong. The owner of the company at fault took my husband to lunch to apologize the very next day. From that lunch, we were able to find the perfect bookkeeper, which we had been diligently seeking for over a year. We also connected with the company in new ways that could benefit us for years to come. That was truly an answered prayer.

The lesson? I need to lighten up. We can all be less angry and learn to laugh more.

I share all this because God has been doing a good work in me to release my so called "right" to righteous anger. When we give up our right to get even, God has space to work within the very situation that upset us in the first place. He has room to bless us in new ways and show us what he can do with our messes when we submit to him in this way. God loves to create beauty out of ashes. And, of course, God redeems what he wants to redeem, whether we give him room or not. But something very powerful can happen when we voluntarily lay down our sword, entrusting the situation to him. It is really remarkable when you experience it happening in real time!

> *Stop being angry! Turn from your rage!*
> *Do not lose your temper—it only leads to harm.*
>
> **PSALM 37:8**

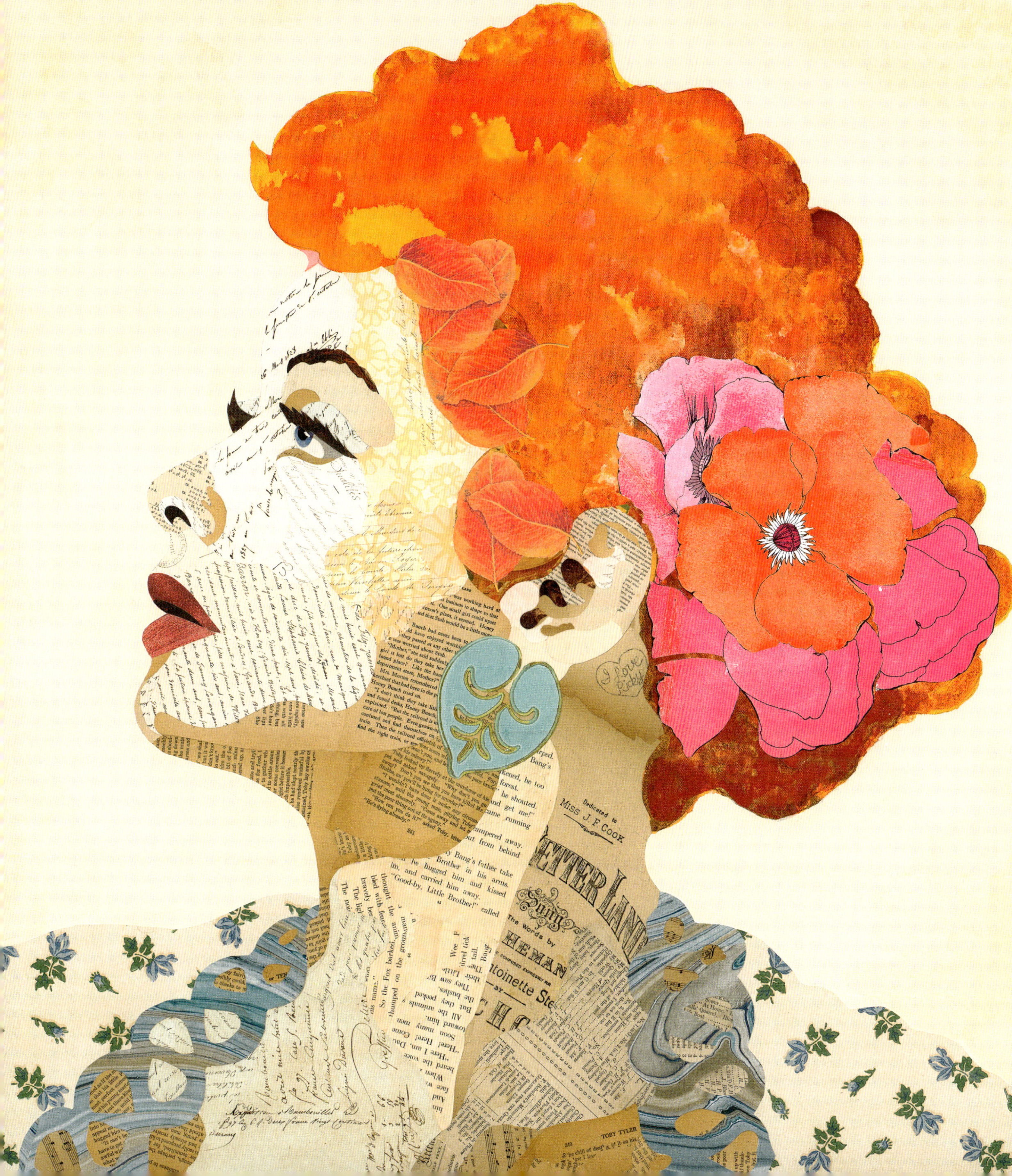

LUCY 3

To all who mourn in Israel, he will give a crown of beauty for ashes, a joyous blessing instead of mourning, festive praise instead of despair. In their righteousness, they will be like great oaks that the Lord has planted for his own glory.

ISAIAH 61:3

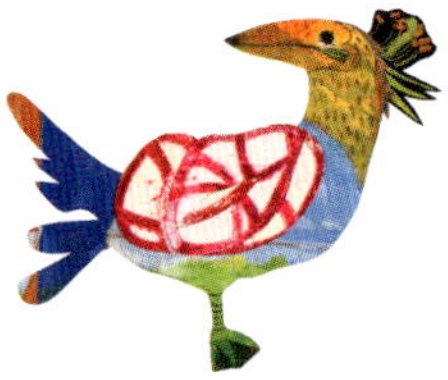

- Why do we feel we have a right to be angry sometimes?
- What can potentially happen if we surrender our right to be upset?

May God lengthen your fuse every passing day.

Don't let the sun go down on your anger.

EPHESIANS 4:26

Choosing the Wrong Shelter.

Those who live in the shelter of the Most High will find rest in the shadow of the Almighty. This I declare about the Lord: He alone is my refuge, my place of safety; he is my God, and I trust him. For he will rescue you from every trap and protect you from deadly disease. He will cover you with his feathers. He will shelter you with his wings. His faithful promises are your armor and protection. Do not be afraid of the terrors of the night, nor the arrow that flies in the day. Do not dread the disease that stalks in darkness, nor the disaster that strikes at midday. Though a thousand fall at your side, though ten thousand are dying around you, these evils will not touch you. Just open your eyes, and see how the wicked are punished. If you make the Lord your refuge, if you make the Most High your shelter, no evil will conquer you; no plague will come near your home. For he will order his angels to protect you wherever you go. They will hold you up with their hands so you won't even hurt your foot on a stone. You will trample upon lions and cobras; you will crush fierce lions and serpents under your feet! The Lord says, "I will rescue those who love me. I will protect those who trust in my name. When they call on me, I will answer; I will be with them in trouble. I will rescue and honor them. I

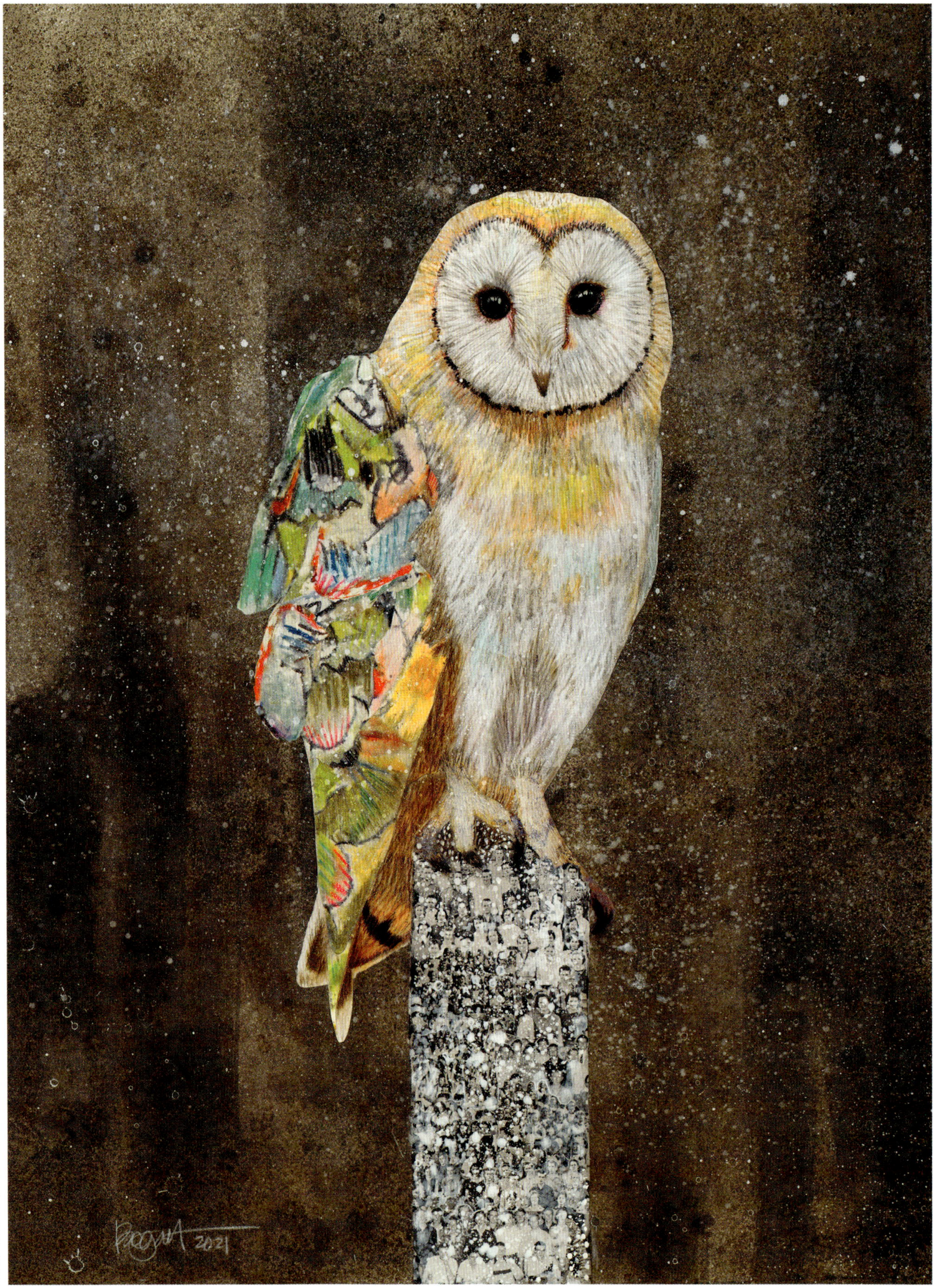

BARN OWL #1 ON A SNOWY NIGHT

will reward them with a long life and give them my salvation."

PSALM 91:1-16

God sometimes gives us sobering reminders about the brevity of life. In one moment, our lives can be unalterably changed.

We all run somewhere for shelter, safety, and security when bad things happen. No matter what comes our way, I know with all my heart that we reside in the shelter of the Almighty, like the Bible describes in Psalm 91. There is no better place to be.

God alone is our refuge and true shelter. Under his wings we find protection from the storms of life that surround each one of us. No matter what terrible or terrifying thing is happening in our lives, in him we can find true rest.

From the ends of the earth, I cry to you for help when my heart is overwhelmed. Lead me to the towering rock of safety, for you are my safe refuge, a fortress where my enemies cannot reach me.

PSALM 61:2-3

You will keep in perfect peace all who trust in you, all whose thoughts are fixed on you!

ISAIAH 26:3

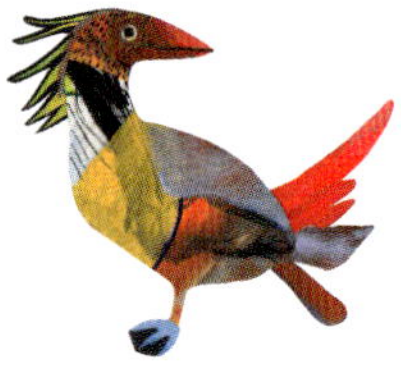

- Where do you typically turn when life goes wrong?
- When was a time you found true shelter in God during one of life's storms?

You are safe in the Lord today.

The name of the Lord is a strong fortress;
the godly run to him and are safe.

PROVERBS 18:10

DAMNING GOD.

You shall not take the name of the Lord your God in vain, for the Lord will not hold him guiltless who takes his name in vain.

EXODUS 20:7 ESV

I never hear anyone damn Buddha in conversation or in movies. I never hear anyone damn Muhammad.

Do you?

Why do people and popular figures so easily damn God in society today? Does hearing this irreverent phrase hurt your heart? Do your friends and colleagues know not to damn God around you? There is no one more sacred than God, and misusing his name is never okay.

You shall not swear by my name falsely, and so profane the name of your God: I am the Lord.

LEVITICUS 19:12 ESV

With all my heart I will praise you, O Lord my God. I will give glory to your name forever.

PSALM 86:12

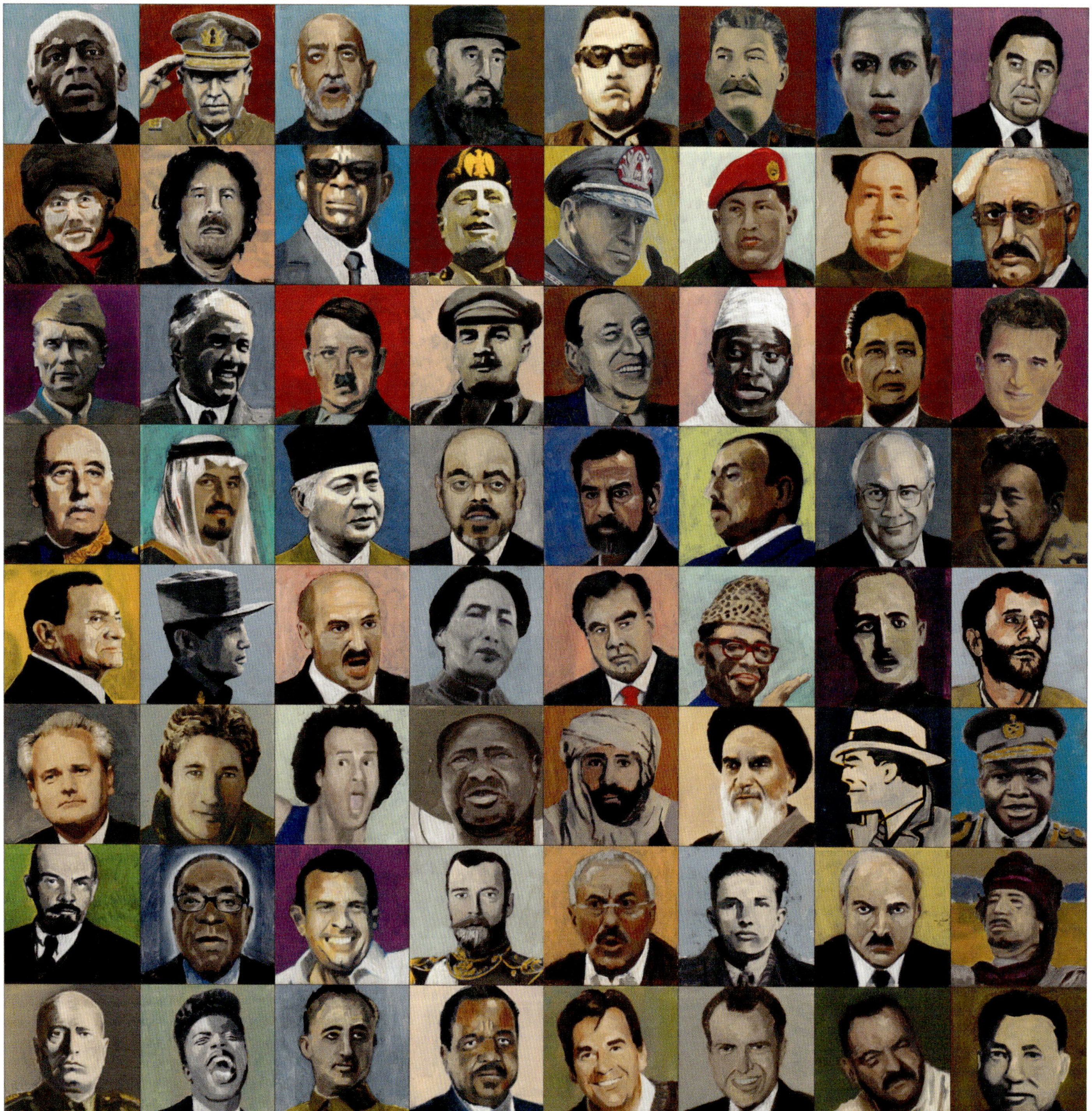

Don't copy the behavior and customs of this world, but let God transform you into a new person by changing the way you think. Then you will learn to know God's will for you, which is good and pleasing and perfect.

ROMANS 12:2

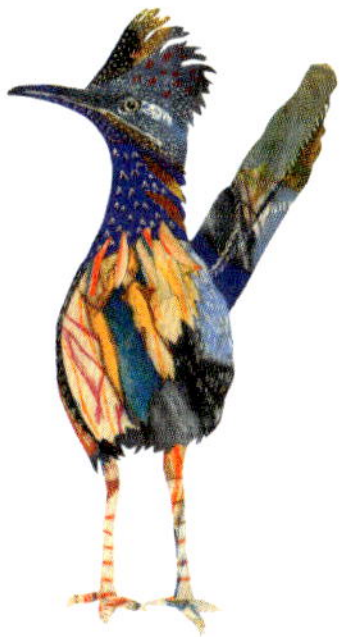

- What bothers you most about the irreverent use of God's name?
- Why do you think our culture readily excuses using God's name in vain?

Take the opportunity to lift high God's name today.

Jesus said...."Father, may your name be kept holy."

LUKE 11:2

A Works-Based Theology.

For you are a holy people, who belong to the Lord your God. Of all the people on earth, the Lord your God has chosen you to be his own special treasure. The Lord did not set his heart on you and choose you because you were more numerous than other nations, for you were the smallest of all nations! Rather, it was simply that the Lord loves you, and he was keeping the oath he had sworn to your ancestors. That is why the Lord rescued you with such a strong hand from your slavery and from the oppressive hand of Pharaoh, king of Egypt. Understand, therefore, that the Lord your God is indeed God. He is the faithful God who keeps his covenant for a thousand generations and lavishes his unfailing love on those who love him and obey his commands.

DEUTERONOMY 7:6-9

"It was simply that the Lord loves you..."

Those words get me every time. It is an overwhelming thought that God chooses to bless us just because he loves us. Here's the deal—a works-based theology separates other religions from Christianity. In Christianity, God came *down* to us. All other religions require us to strive *upward* toward God. Christianity is based on faith in

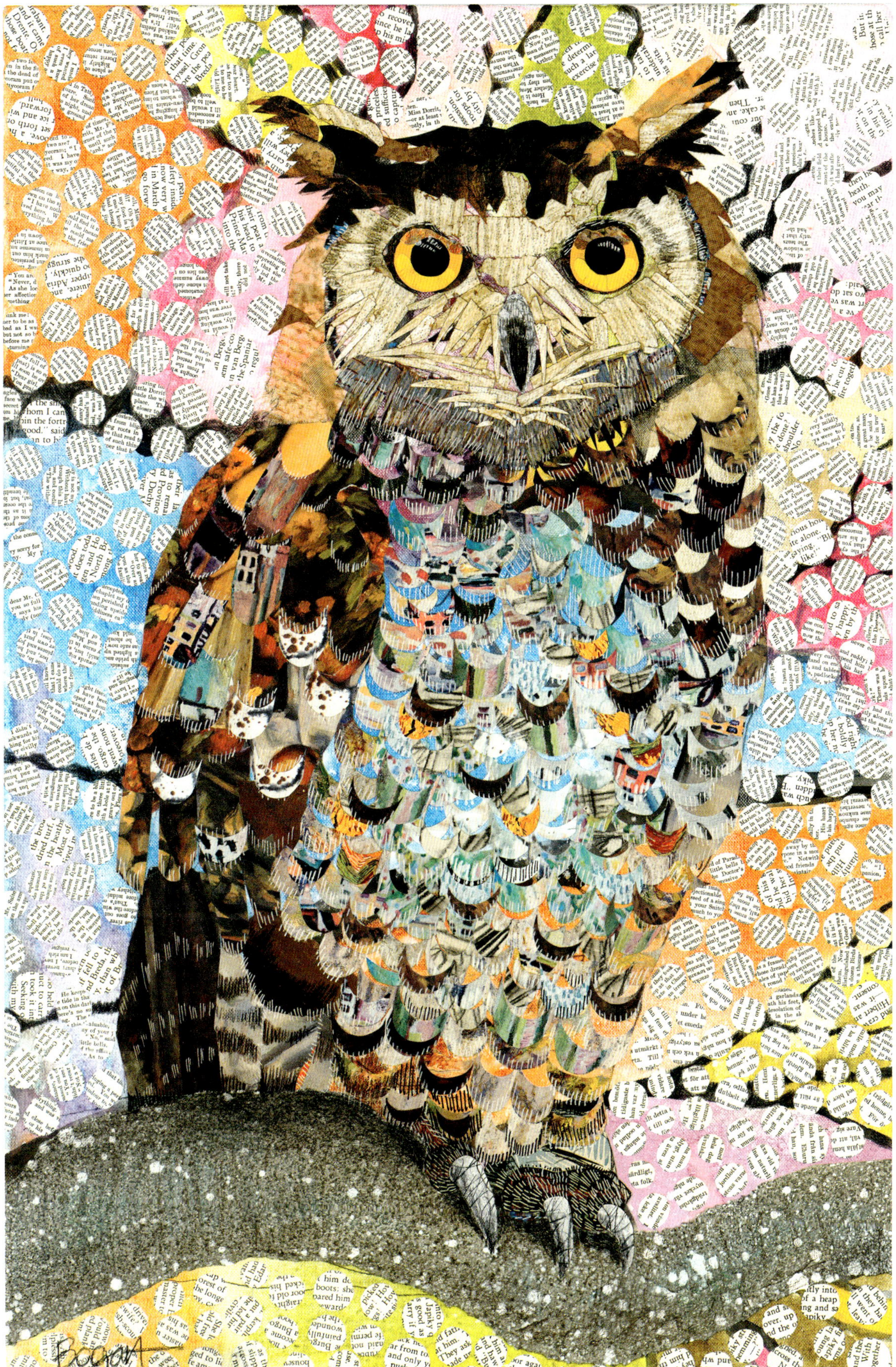

EAGLE OWL

God's unmerited, unearned grace *gifted* to humanity and earned only by Christ's voluntary work on the cross and his resurrection.

That's why we follow Christ, not other Christians. Remember what Jesus said to impetuous Peter when he was comparing himself to the other disciples? Jesus simply and emphatically said, "Peter, *you* follow *me!*"

Here are some additional grace-based truths I see in this passage from Deuteronomy after I spent time meditating on it and reading it in several translations:

"You were chosen"

"You belong to me"

"I chose you to be my own special treasure"

"My love for you is not based on who you are or what you do"

"You cannot earn my love"

"My *heart* is set on *you*"

"You, yes you, matter to me"

"I freed you from the iron grip of slavery"

"I redeemed you from the house of slavery"

"I did this out of sheer love, not because you are a big deal"

"I am stronger than your sin"

"I am indeed God"

"I am the faithful one"

"I keep my covenant"

"It is impossible for me to break a promise"

"My love will never fail you"

"You can depend on me"

"I lavish my love on those who love me and obey me"

"I love you because of who I am, not because of what you do"

"My loving kindness is steadfast"

"I will bless your obedience, but no matter what, I will always love you"

What do you see? For more about grace versus works, read Galatians chapter 2 and the Book of John.

> *Yet we know that a person is made right with God by faith in Jesus Christ, not by obeying the law. And we have believed in Christ Jesus, so that we might be made right with God because of our faith in Christ, not because we have obeyed the law. For no one will ever be made right with God by obeying the law. I do not treat the grace of God as meaningless. For if keeping the law could make us right with God, then there was no need for Christ to die.*
>
> **GALATIANS 2:16, 21**

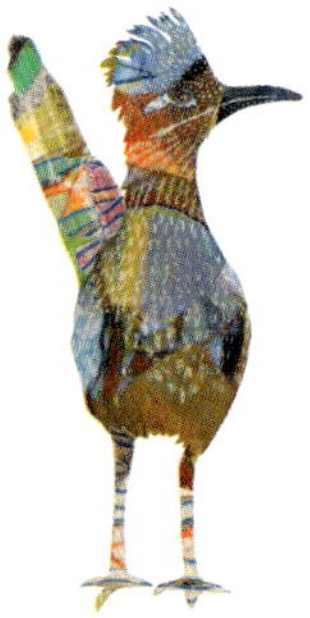

- What is your definition of grace?
- Why are people tempted to work to earn God's love?

May God enfold you in his grace today.

And he gives grace generously.

JAMES 4:6

Religiosity.

I want you to show love, not offer sacrifices. I want you to know me more than I want burnt offerings.

HOSEA 6:6

Some people are famous for not sticking to the rules.

Did you know that God prefers a relationship over rules and rituals? He wants our heart more than our empty religious deeds. God desires deeply to be known by us.

God is not saying that we should stop going to church or stop taking communion. Those practices are there for a reason. We need them. We need to remember. They nourish us spiritually. But above all, he wants our love. God wants a relationship with us here and now, on this side of heaven. Ask him to show you more of who he is. Seek him with all your heart. I encourage you to read slowly through the Book of John while you pray for him to show you who he really is.

What is more pleasing to the Lord: your burnt offerings and sacrifices or your obedience to his Word?

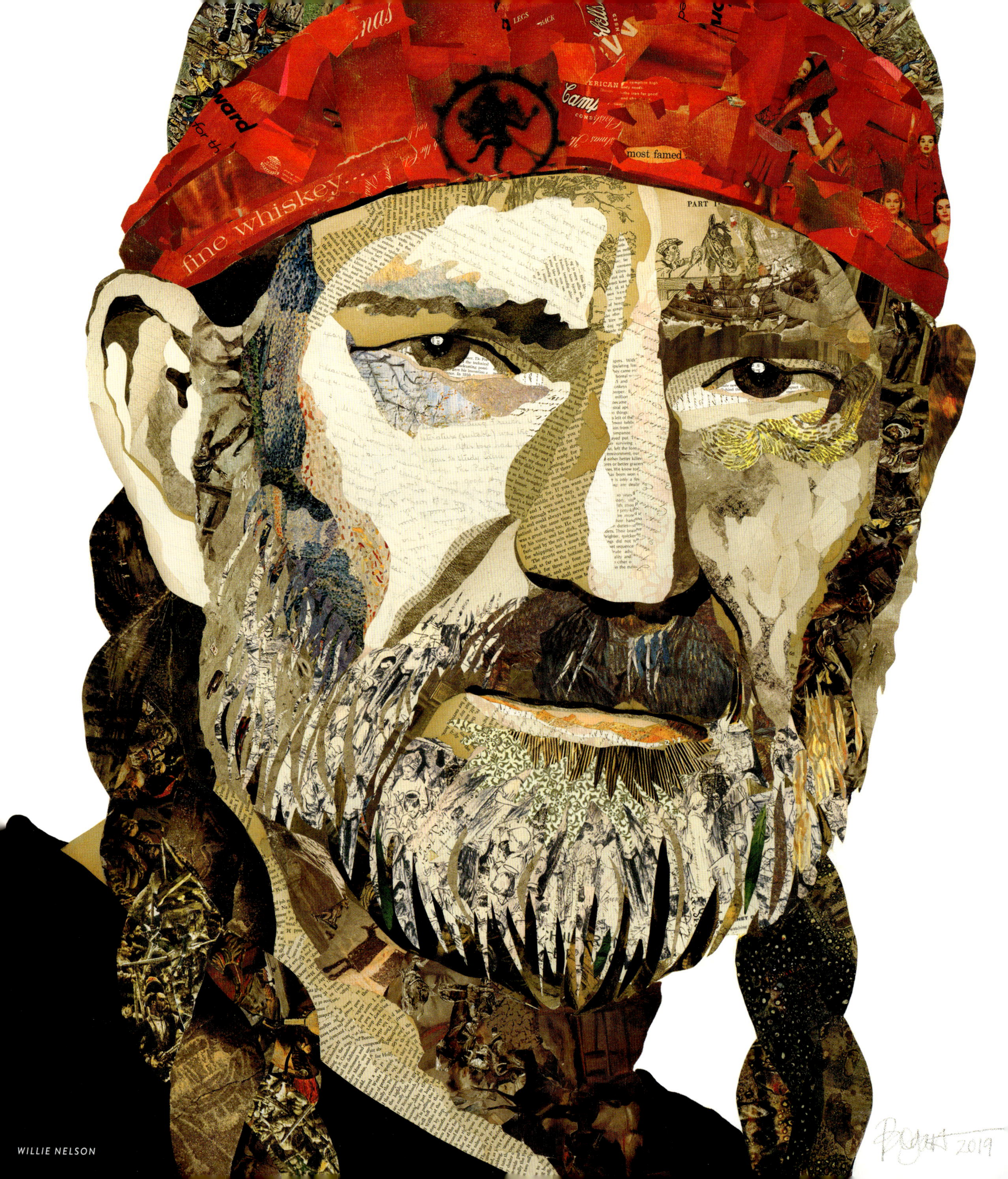

WILLIE NELSON

Listen! Obedience is better than sacrifice...

1 SAMUEL 15:22

The Lord isn't really being slow about his promise, as some people think. No, he is being patient for your sake. He does not want anyone to be destroyed, but wants everyone to repent.

2 PETER 3:9

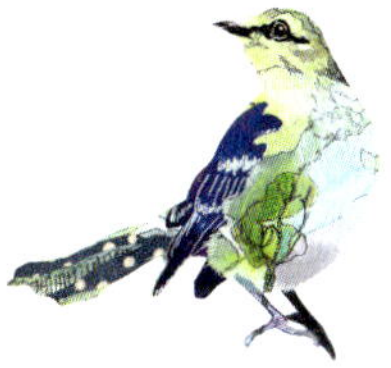

- What is the difference between religion and a relationship with God?
- Based on your experience, how would you describe who God is to someone else?

Relax! It's by God's grace, not rules.

Salvation is not a reward for the good things we have done, so none of us can boast about it.

EPHESIANS 2:9

NOT SHARING MYSELF.

Let me proclaim your power to this new generation,
your mighty miracles to all who come after me.

PSALM 71:18

When I was asked to be the "Big Brothers Big Sisters" artist of the year, my charge was to create a piece of art that depicted mentoring and coincided with the theme: "An Evening of Masterpieces." The inspiration for this piece is certainly the little vignette of Picasso's 1954 painting, *Claude dessinant, Francoise et Paloma*, featuring a woman teaching two children how to draw. I admire how masterfully Picasso captures the act of mentoring and teaching in this painting. The overall theme of "big and little" is further depicted by the two trees. One tree, much larger and stronger, appears to shield and shade the younger, smaller tree. The little tree is quite healthy and full of color. This profusion of happy color represents the joy the "littles" take in when they receive that rarest of all gifts—someone taking time to notice and encourage them. That's the essence of mentoring.

I have invested much of my time in mentoring over the years. It requires commitment and emotional energy to help younger generations connect with God's unique purpose for their lives. "What do *you* want to do?" is the first question I usually ask. I was an adult before I had the courage to pursue my true passion—and

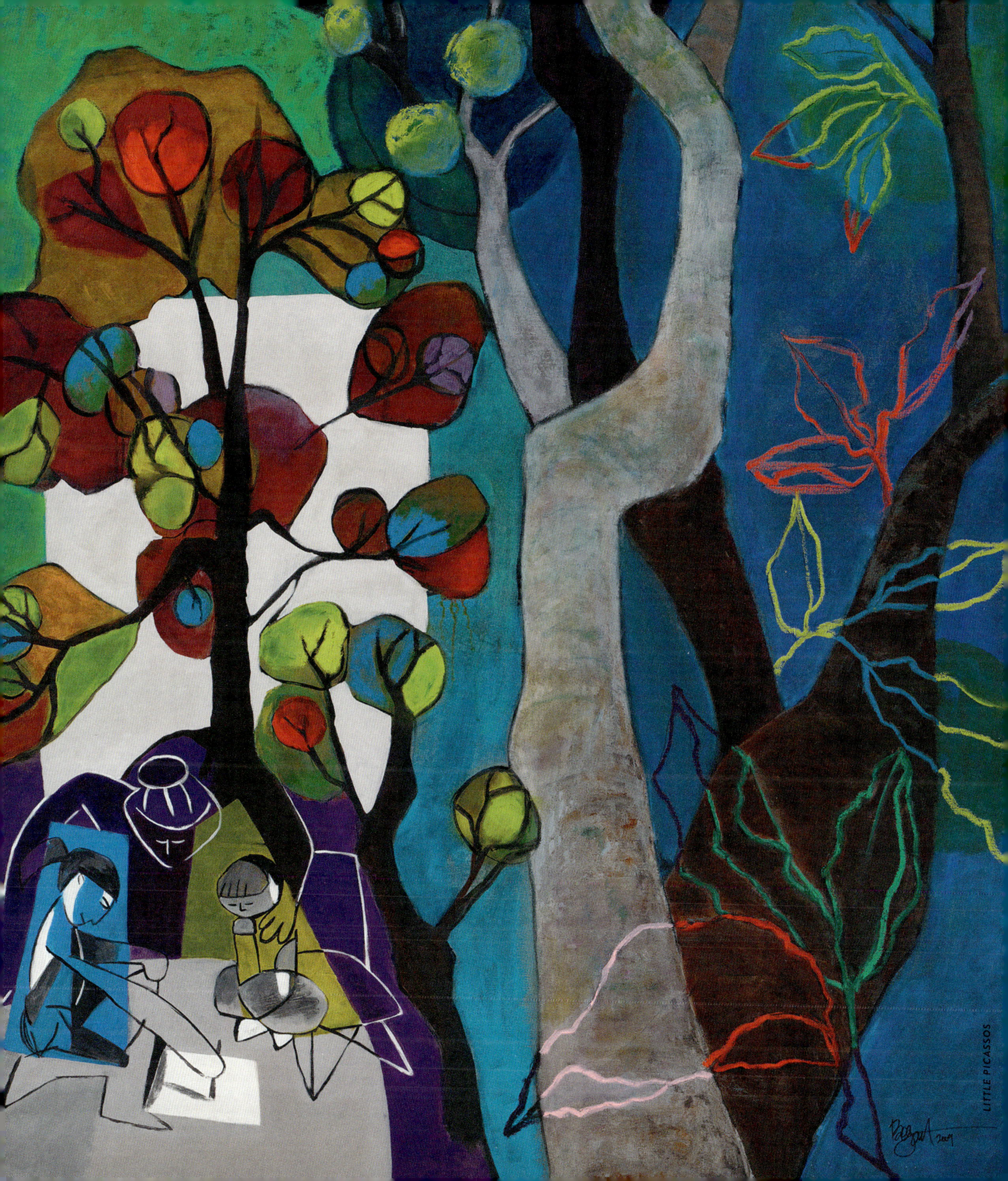

I lost a lot of time trying to make others happy. As children, we often lose our own identity in trying to please others. I know I wanted to please my parents more than anything. They have always wanted the best for me and and have showered me with their time, love, and resources. But I spent most of my life pursuing *their* approval above focusing on what God had created me to be. Had I gotten this right, I would have found my passion and purpose much sooner.

It's *our* responsibility to discover the buried treasure within that God has planted inside each of us to enable and equip us to fulfill our unique purpose. And then we can encourage someone else to do the same. The incomprehensible thought that we are all uniquely fashioned by our Creator gives great importance to the responsibility to pursue my individual calling. And what a positive message we can then share with someone we're mentoring: "No one else who has ever lived can do what you do, in the way you do it."

For example, I have a longtime friend who is such a great listener and a very generous person. She never fails to celebrate each and every milestone in the seemingly zillions of friends in her circle. It is impressive to watch and experience. Her heart is so big. She has this unique capacity to feel empathy and love for a very large number of close friends. It is astounding and overwhelming to me, but it comes so effortlessly from her. She is not even aware how unique her gift is.

In the same way, I am to glorify, know, and enjoy God by using the special gifts and talents that he gave me—in a combination that is unique to me! And I can help others do the same. So, let me ask you: What do *you* want to do? And how might you help someone else find the answer to that question?

We loved you so much that we shared with you not only God's Good News but our own lives, too.

1 THESSALONIANS 2:8

Let the message about Christ, in all its richness, fill your lives. Teach and counsel each other with all the wisdom he gives. Sing psalms and hymns and spiritual songs to God with thankful hearts.

COLOSSIANS 3:16

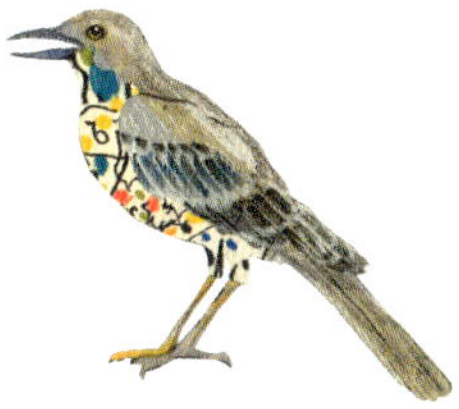

- What do you feel you were "made" to do? What things give you energy?
- How can you help someone younger find their purpose in life?

Find your gifts—and help others find theirs.

One generation shall commend your works to another, and shall declare your mighty acts.

PSALM 145:4 ESV

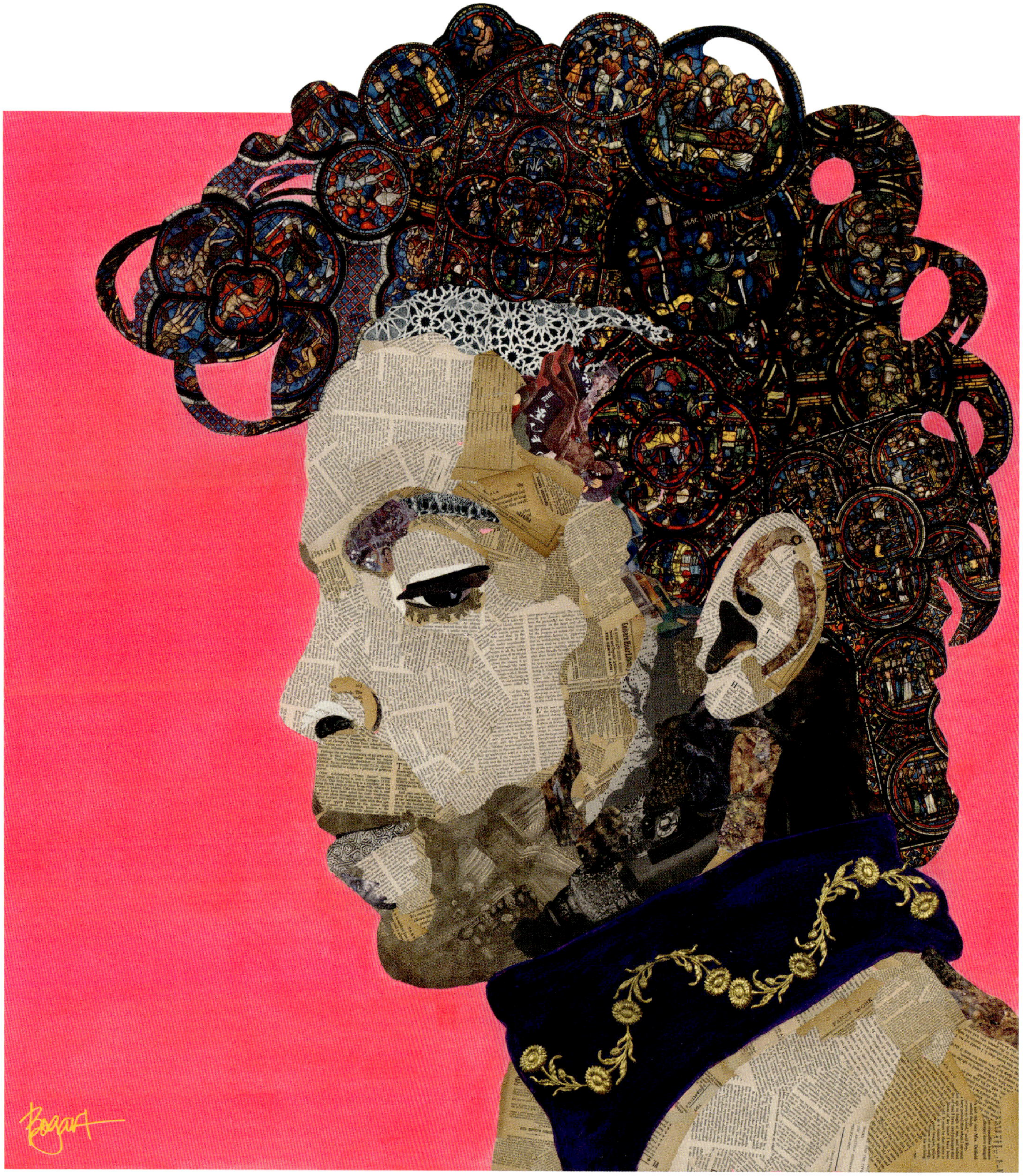

PRINCE

Doubting God's Power to Redeem.

I am deeply grateful to our Lord Jesus Christ (to whom I owe all that I have accomplished) for trusting me enough to appoint me his minister, despite the fact that I had previously blasphemed his name, persecuted his Church and damaged his cause. I believe he was merciful to me because what I did was done in the ignorance of a man without faith, and then he poured out his grace upon me, giving me tremendous faith in, and love for, himself. This statement is completely reliable and should be universally accepted:—"Christ Jesus entered the world to rescue sinners." I realize that I was the worst of them all, and that because of this very fact God was particularly merciful to me. It was a kind of demonstration of the extent of Christ's patience towards the worst of men, to serve as an example to all who in the future should trust him for eternal life.

1 TIMOTHY 1:12-16 PME

Prior to encountering Jesus on the road to Damascus, Saul (renamed Paul) terrorized and persecuted Christians. He even stood by, watching with approval as they were murdered for their belief in Christ—and he did so in the name of honoring God. But God transformed him into the Apostle Paul, arguably the most impactful Christian of all time.

What does that mean he can do with me? When we doubt God's unlimited power to redeem anyone and anything, we wonder if he can truly forgive us and still use us regardless of what's transpired in the past.

Believe it or not, if we just ask, he can! Remember, God's power to redeem is greater than our worst sin. And that's the kind of message that's music to our ears.

> *He is so rich in kindness and grace that he purchased our freedom with the blood of his Son and forgave our sins.*
>
> **EPHESIANS 1:7**

> *I have swept away your sins like a cloud. I have scattered your offenses like the morning mist. Oh, return to me, for I have paid the price to set you free.*
>
> **ISAIAH 44:22**

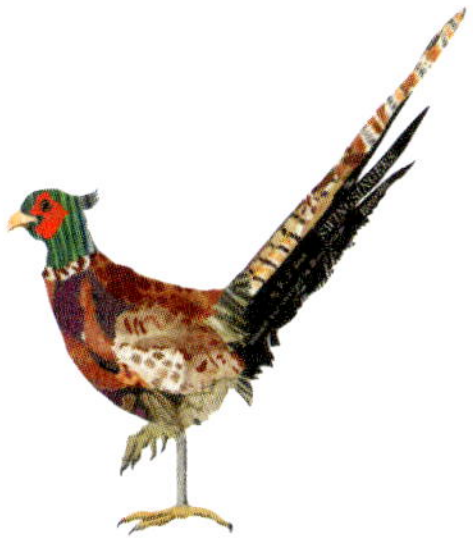

- What does it mean to you to be "redeemed"?
- What does doubt do to our faith?

You. Are. Forgiven.

For God so loved the world that he gave his one and only Son, that whoever believes in him shall not perish but have eternal life.

JOHN 3:16 NIV

Lack of Discernment.

Dear friends, do not believe everyone who claims to speak by the Spirit. You must test them to see if the spirit they have comes from God. For there are many false prophets in the world. This is how we know if they have the Spirit of God: If a person claiming to be a prophet acknowledges that Jesus Christ came in a real body, that person has the Spirit of God. But if someone claims to be a prophet and does not acknowledge the truth about Jesus, that person is not from God. Such a person has the spirit of the Antichrist, which you heard is coming into the world and indeed is already here. But you belong to God, my dear children. You have already won a victory over those people, because the Spirit who lives in you is greater than the spirit who lives in the world.

1 JOHN 4:1-4

The night of Jesus' trial (that ultimately sent him to the cross), there was a gross lack of discernment among many people. The religious and government officials listened to the crowd, not to the facts. The crowd listened to the growing-like-wildfire popular opinion.

Who has our ear? Are they filled with godly wisdom? How do we know who is right

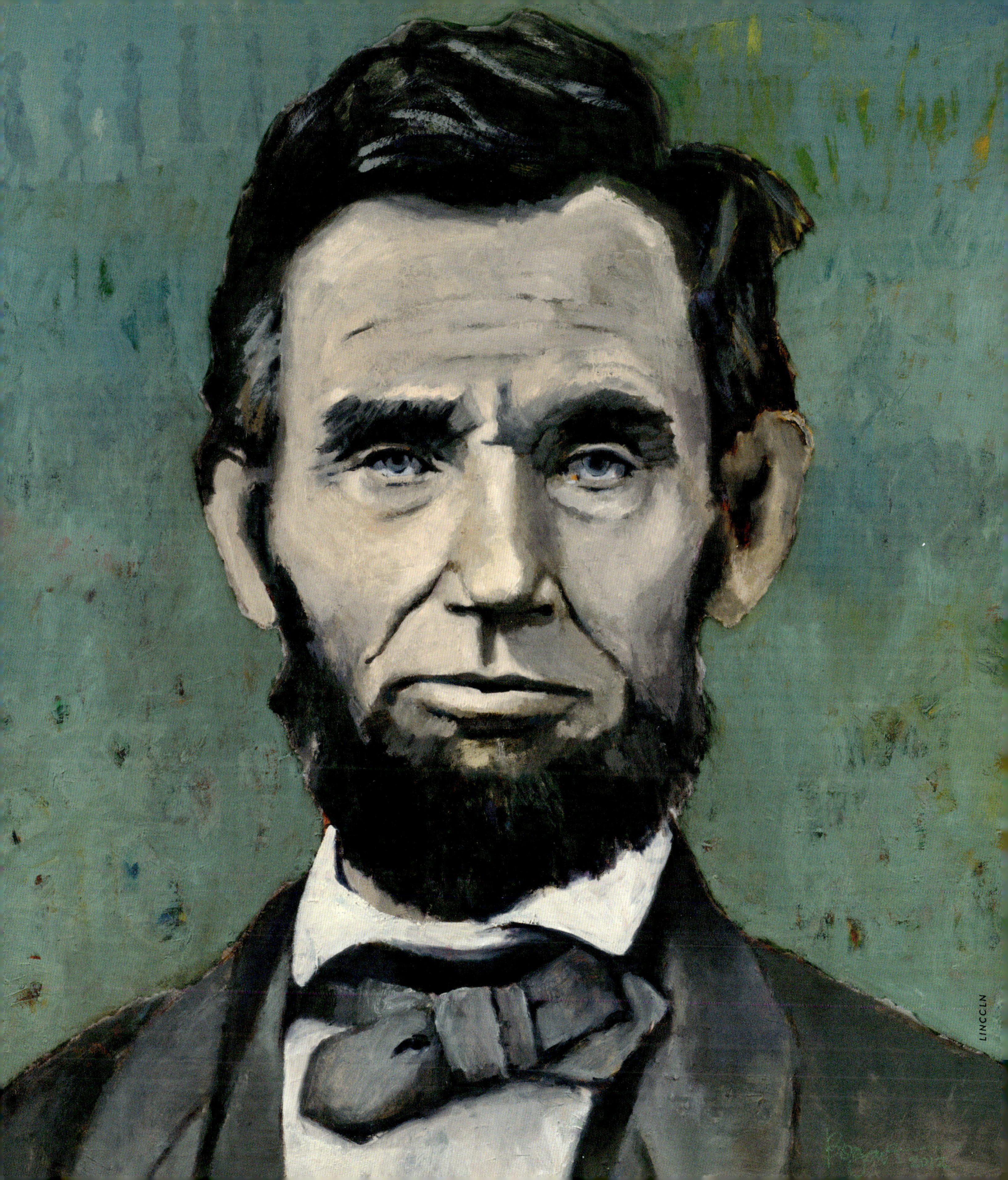

LINCOLN

and who is wrong? Throughout history, wise leaders have made crucial decisions that often went against popular opinion. There may be times in our lives when we are called to make decisions that could affect many people's lives down the line. We need to be wise. Discernment is a practiced skill.

Sometimes the crowd gets it wrong. But God made it right.

> *I pray that your love will overflow more and more, and that you will keep on growing in knowledge and understanding.*
>
> **PHILIPPIANS 1:9**

> *But people who aren't spiritual can't receive these truths from God's Spirit. It all sounds foolish to them and they can't understand it, for only those who are spiritual can understand what the Spirit means.*
>
> **1 CORINTHIANS 2:14**

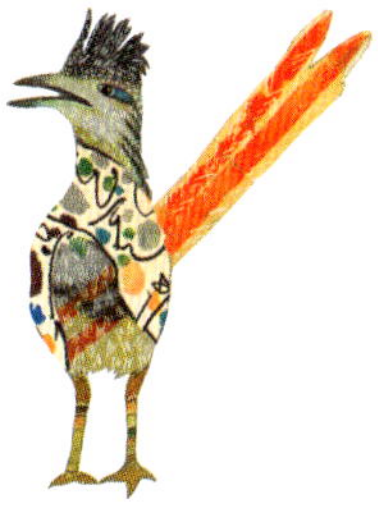

- How would you define wisdom and discernment in your own words?
- Who influences you in the most important decisions in your life?

May God make us wiser than our years.

...but test everything that is said. Hold on to what is good.

1 THESSALONIANS 5:21

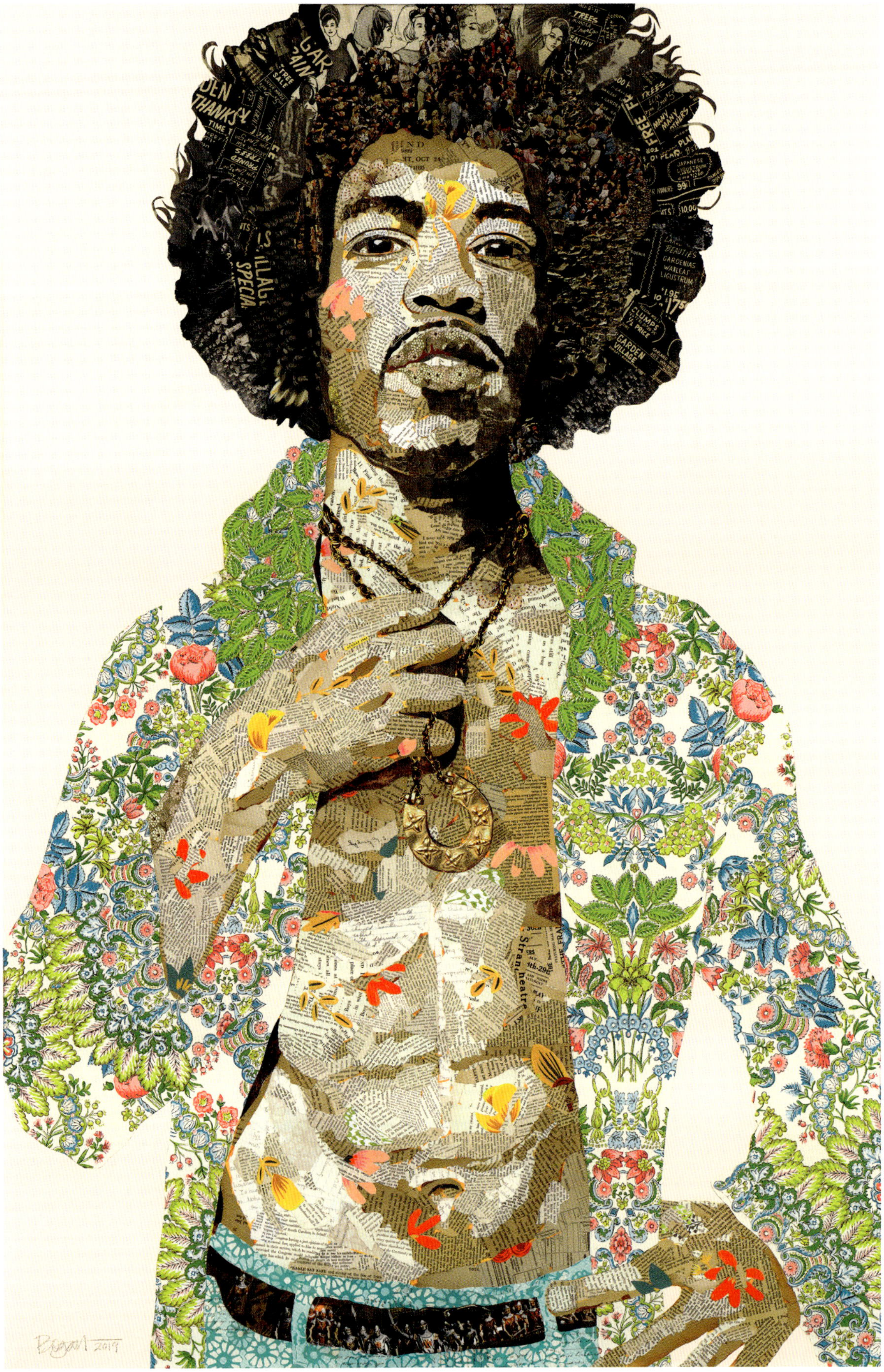

JIMI HENDRIX

A SPIRIT OF POVERTY.

And this same God who takes care of me will supply all your needs from his glorious riches, which have been given to us in Christ Jesus.

PHILIPPIANS 4:19

What does it mean to give up a spirit of poverty? I decided to ask myself some questions to find out.

Do I resent the wealthy? Do I look down on the poor? Do I criticize people for spending the money they have, making offhand comments like, "They should have spent their money on this instead of that"? Am I stingy, discontent, or dissatisfied with all that I have?

Sometimes the answer to all these questions is "yes."

And this could mean that I have a spirit of poverty. Money is not our enemy. It's the lust for money that gets us in trouble. My value is not found in my possessions, but in my relationship with Jesus. A wonderful sense of contentment can take the place of a spirit of poverty when we have the right perspective on money and possessions.

Don't love money; be satisfied with what you have. For God has said, "I will never fail you. I will never abandon you."

HEBREWS 13:5

For wherever there is jealousy and selfish ambition, there you will find disorder and evil of every kind.

JAMES 3:16

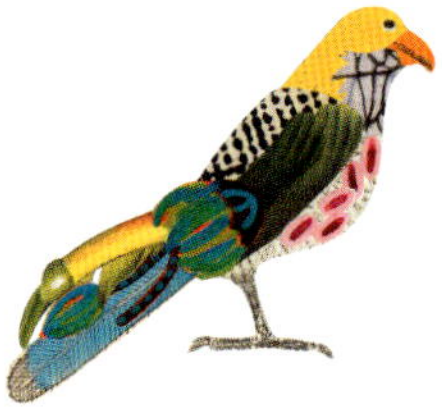

- What are the greatest benefits of being content in life?
- How would you describe the best attitude we can have toward money?

Be content with all you have.

But seek first the kingdom of God and his righteousness, and all these things will be added to you.

MATTHEW 6:33 ESV

Giving in to Temptation.

No temptation has overtaken you that is not common to man. God is faithful, and he will not let you be tempted beyond your ability, but with the temptation he will also provide the way of escape, that you may be able to endure it.

1 CORINTHIANS 10:13 ESV

Here are some tips I use whenever I am tempted to do something I shouldn't:

Say out loud, "Jesus help me!"

Just say no.

Walk away.

Count to 100.

Take 20 deep breaths.

Tell myself I can get through the next 30 minutes.

You can also memorize powerful scriptures, including 1 Corinthians 10:13. Remember, God *always* provides a way out when you are tempted to do or say

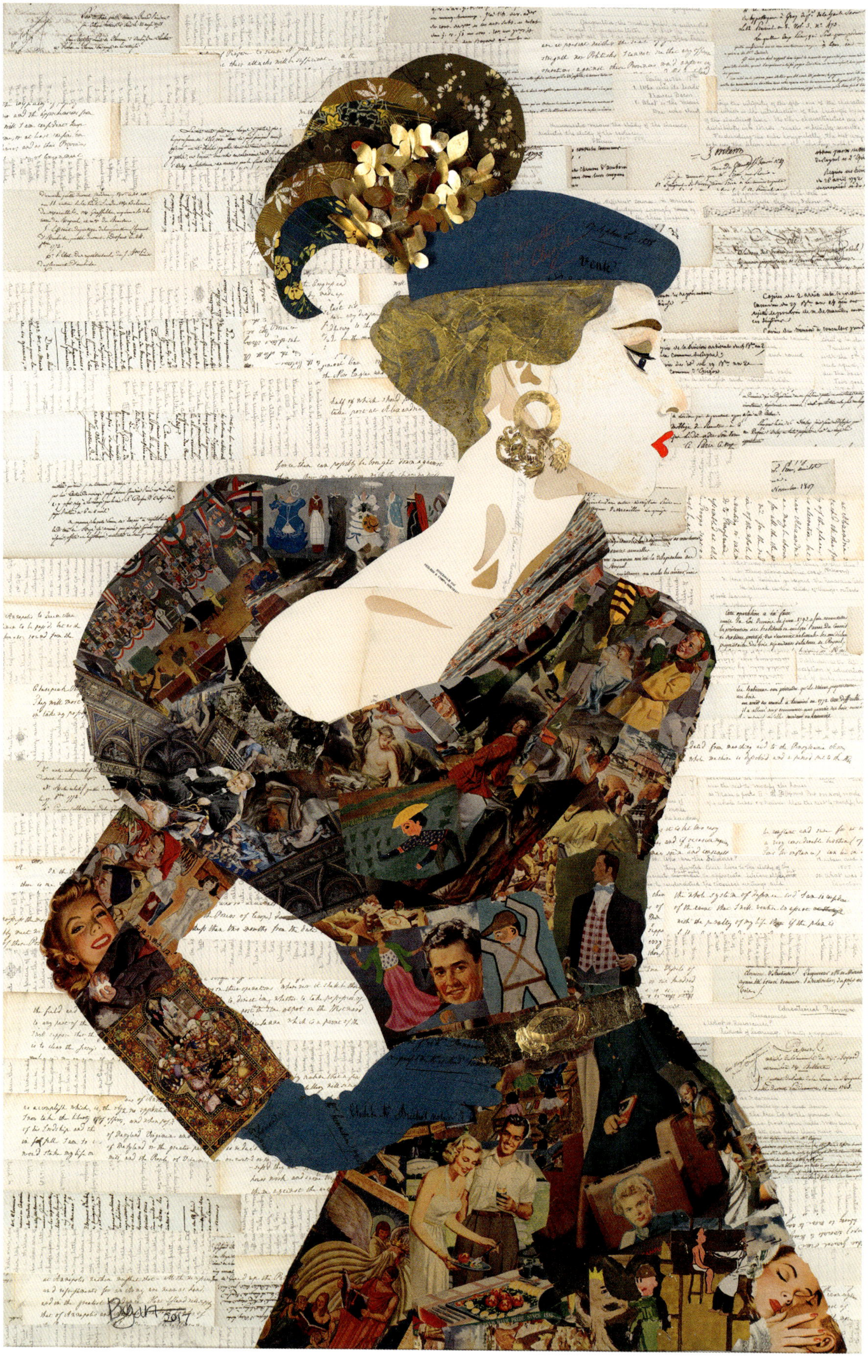

WOMAN WITH BLUE HAT

something wrong. Ask him to help you see the exit door and make your way out of the situation.

Keep watch and pray, so that you will not give in to temptation. For the spirit is willing, but the body is weak.

MARK 14:38

Since he himself has gone through suffering and testing, he is able to help us when we are being tested.

HEBREWS 2:18

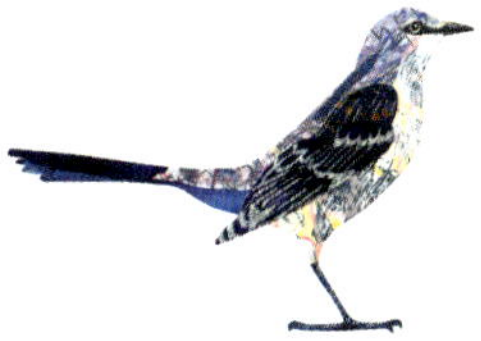

- Name some common temptations people face every day.
- What is the best strategy for overcoming temptation?

Be strong in the Lord today.

Finally, be strong in the Lord and in the strength of his might.

EPHESIANS 6:10

Gossip.

Let everything you say be good and helpful, so that your words will be an encouragement to those who hear them.

EPHESIANS 4:29

Listening to gossip is as harmful as delivering it. Trying to undo the damage of gossip is like standing on top of a windy hill and shaking feathers out of a pillow, then running around trying to gather every single feather to put back in the pillow. It is a futile effort!

A troublemaker plants seeds of strife; gossip separates the best of friends.

PROVERBS 16:28

The mouth of the righteous is a fountain of life...

PROVERBS 10:11 ESV

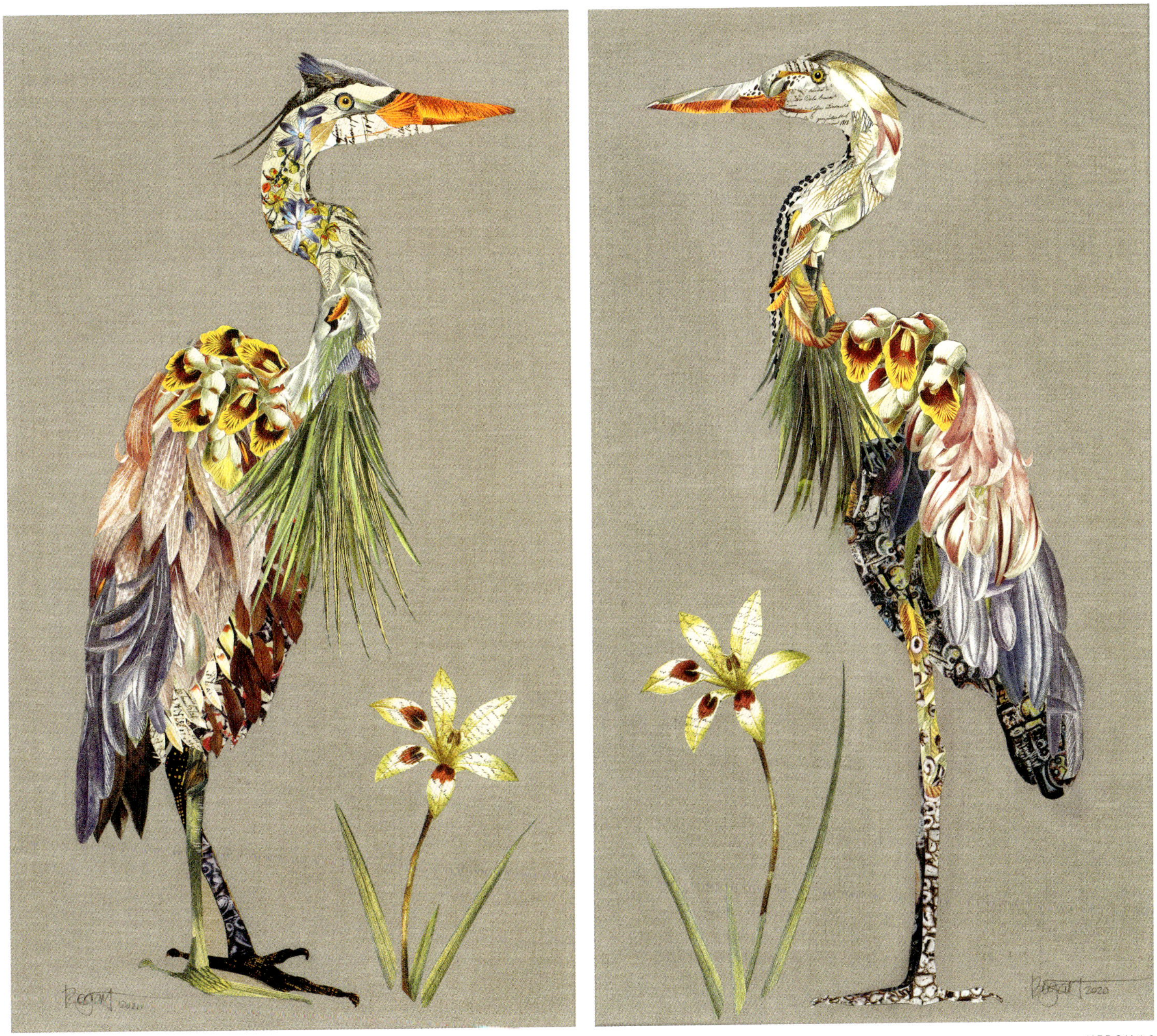

HERON 1,2

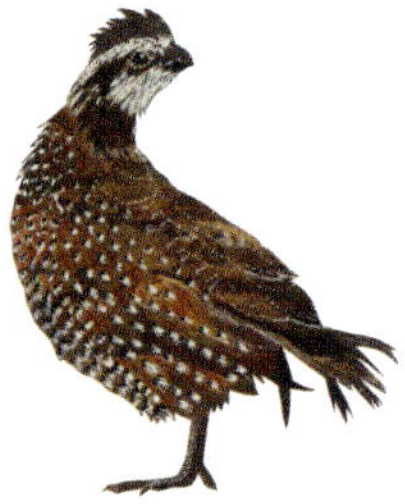

- Why do people naturally want to gossip about others?
- How can you develop a reputation for keeping confidences, not gossiping?

May it never be said of you that you are a gossip.

A gossip goes around telling secrets,
but those who are trustworthy can keep a confidence.

PROVERBS 11:13

Lack of Courage.

Have I not commanded you? Be strong and courageous. Do not be frightened, and do not be dismayed, for the Lord your God is with you wherever you go.

JOSHUA 1:9 ESV

Winston Churchill's famous speech to a class of British schoolboys in 1941 was short and sweet: "Never give in! Never give in! Never, never, never, never..."

I have something to add to that: Take courage! Whatever you are afraid of, our God is stronger! When I made the big, bold move to return to the classroom in my mid-40s to pursue a career in art, my husband had to practically push me out the door that first day. I had already accomplished much in the world's eyes concerning my career, but nothing frightened me like pursuing this long-held desire and facing the failure I might encounter on the other side of that proverbial door. The fear literally paralyzed me.

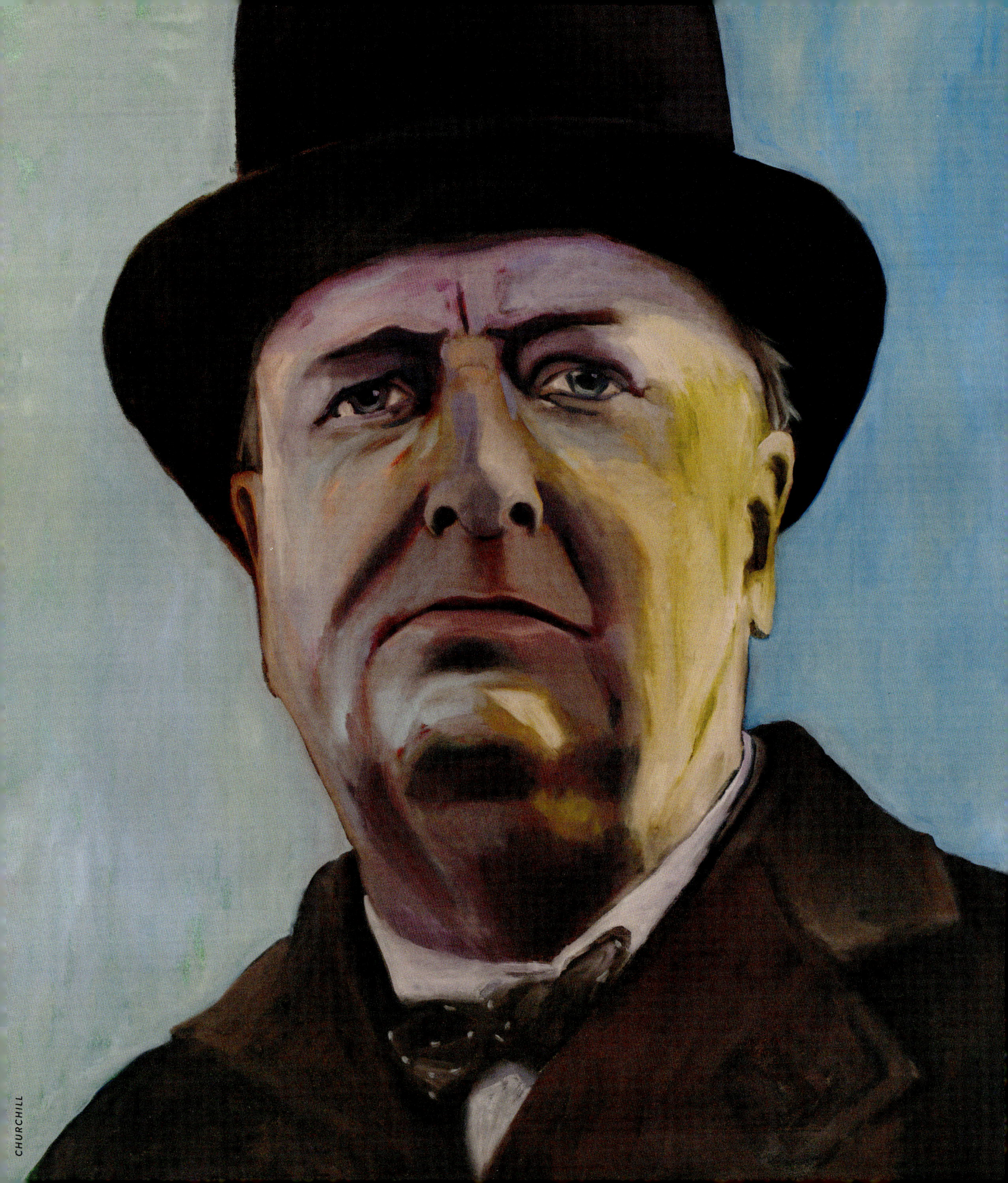

CHURCHILL

For I, the Lord your God, hold your right hand; it is I who say to you, "Fear not, I am the one who helps you."

ISAIAH 41:13

Be on guard. Stand firm in the faith. Be courageous. Be strong.

1 CORINTHIANS 16:13

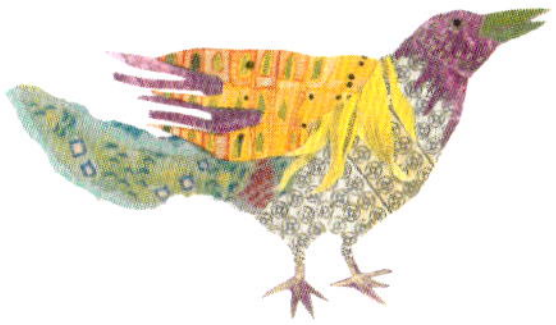

- What do we stand to gain if we stop being afraid in life?
- What kinds of situations or relationships require us to be courageous?

Stand strong in love today.

"Don't be afraid!"

LUKE 2:10

FROWNING.

Restore our fortunes, Lord, as streams renew the desert.

PSALM 126:4

Are you suffering from lack of joy? Have you lost your ability to smile through life? You're not alone. When situations try to steal my joy, here is what I know:

We will get through the darkness.

The dark will turn to light.

God will restore and renew us.

Best of all, just like Christ conquered death and burst victoriously out of a dark cave on Easter morning, we too will be saved from death and reunited with our loved ones.

Some people have a signature look that sets them apart—and sometimes it even makes them famous. Joy ought to be a Christian's signature look. As they say, "A smile is a frown turned upside down." We hurt, but may we never lose hope. Here is my prayer and blessing for you: "I pray that God, the source of hope, will fill you completely with joy and peace because you trust in him. Then you will overflow with confident hope through the power of the Holy Spirit." Romans 15:13

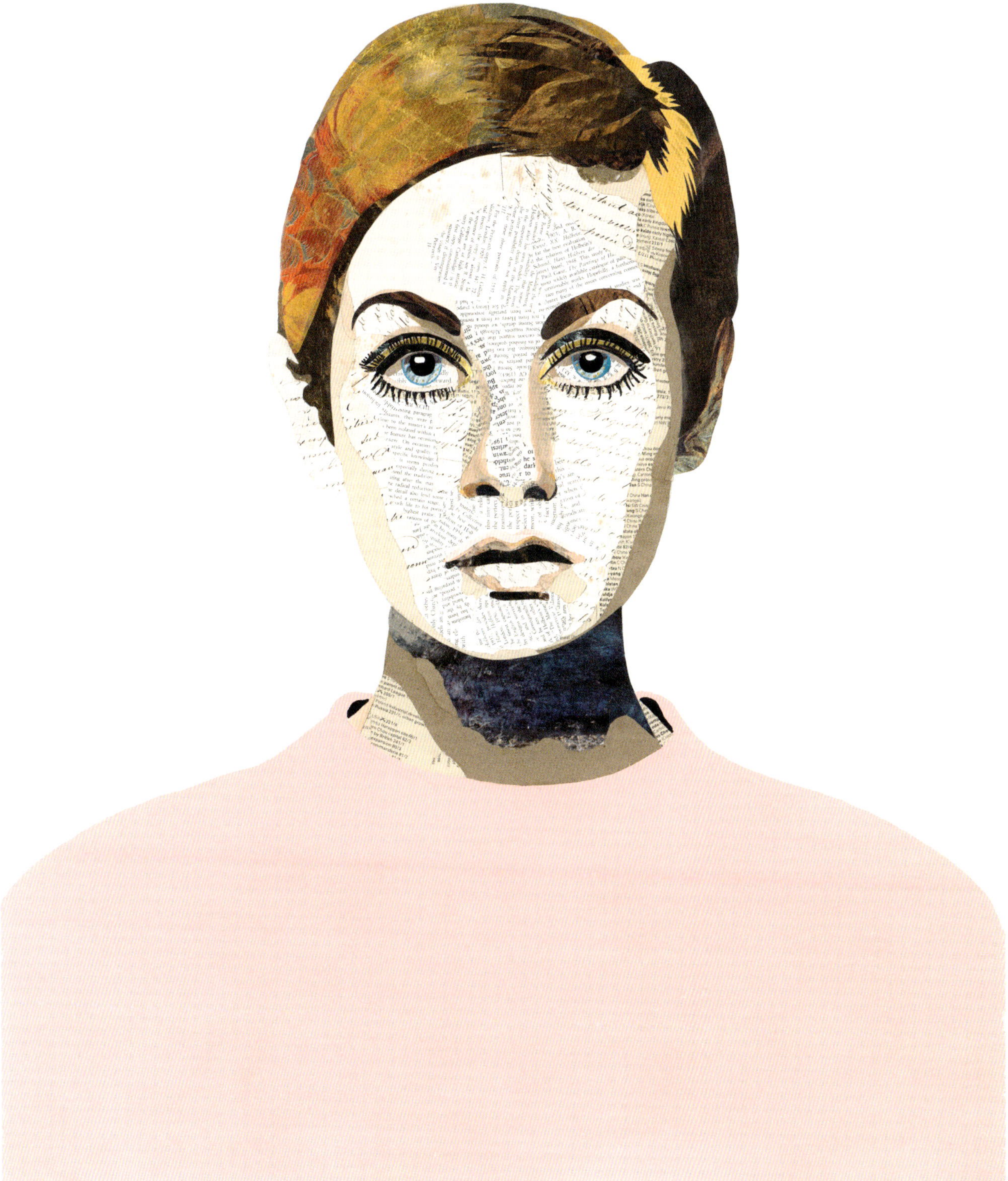

TWIGGY

This is the *hope* you can be confident in! Look how many great phrases are in this verse:

#sourceofhope #joyandpeace #becauseyoutrust #trustinhim #overflowwithhope #confidenthope #throughthepower #holyspiritpower

Did you know hashtagging a verse is a form of meditation? Me neither, until I learned to do it! It's a great exercise to do whenever you are feeling like you're losing your joy in the middle of a situation. Do you see more insights to hashtag in any of these scriptures?

He will once again fill your mouth with laughter
and your lips with shouts of joy.

JOB 8:21

Rejoice in hope, be patient in tribulation, be constant in prayer.

ROMANS 12:12 ESV

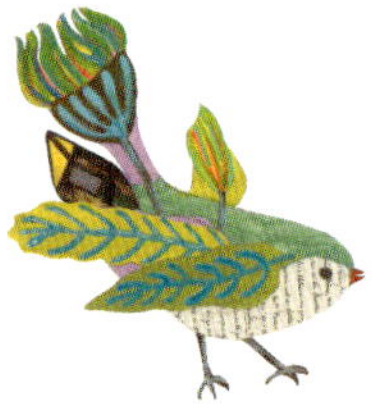

- What brings you the most joy?
- What situations or relationships try to steal your joy?

God's joy will pull you through.

For nothing will be impossible with God.

LUKE 1:37 ESV

Denying God's Greatest Gift.

In the beginning was the Word, and the Word was with God, and the Word was God. He was in the beginning with God. All things were made through him, and without him was not any thing made that was made. In him was life, and the life was the light of men. The light shines in the darkness, and the darkness has not overcome it.

He came to his own, and his own people did not receive him. But to all who did receive him, who believed in his name, he gave the right to become children of God, who were born, not of blood nor of the will of the flesh nor of the will of man, but of God.

For from his fullness we have all received, grace upon grace. For the law was given through Moses; grace and truth came through Jesus Christ.

JOHN 1:1-5, 11-13, 16-17 ESV

From Genesis to Revelation is the underlying story of God's plan to restore the relationship of his people to himself through his gift of grace. Jesus came voluntarily down to Earth, not to condemn us, but to restore us. To be the fulfillment of God's perfect plan.

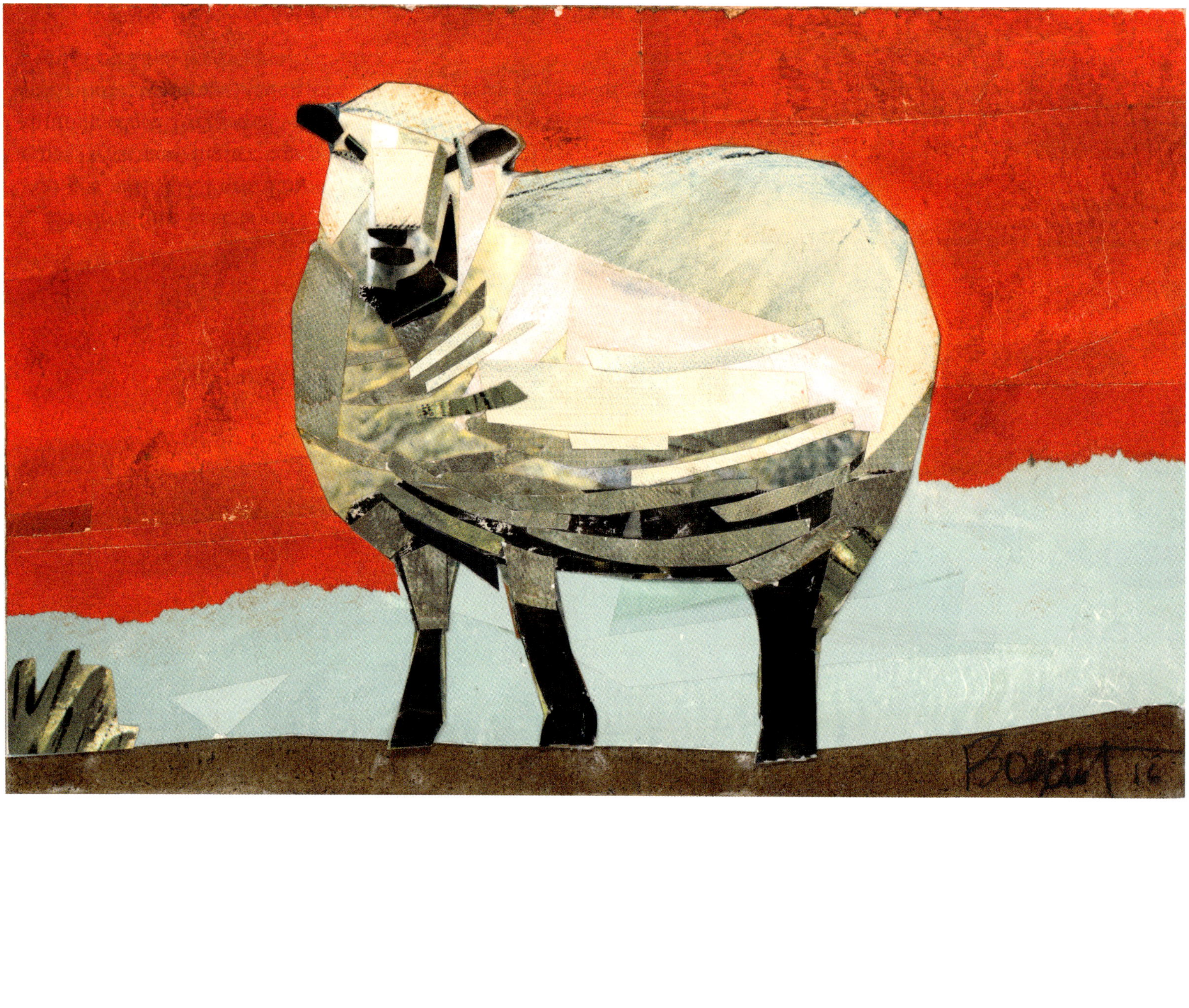

MELISSA'S LAMB

The Holy Spirit is the one who relentlessly pursues us and woos us back to God. To deny this gift, the greatest gift of all gifts, is to deny the one and only thing we truly need. Don't refuse the gift! Instead, receive it! As you look ahead to celebrating Easter, may the God of hope fill you with a renewed sense of joy and peace.

He has delivered us from the domain of darkness and transferred us to the kingdom of his beloved Son, in whom we have redemption, the forgiveness of sins.

COLOSSIANS 1:13-14 ESV

And walk in love, as Christ loved us and gave himself up for us, a fragrant offering and sacrifice to God.

EPHESIANS 5:2 ESV

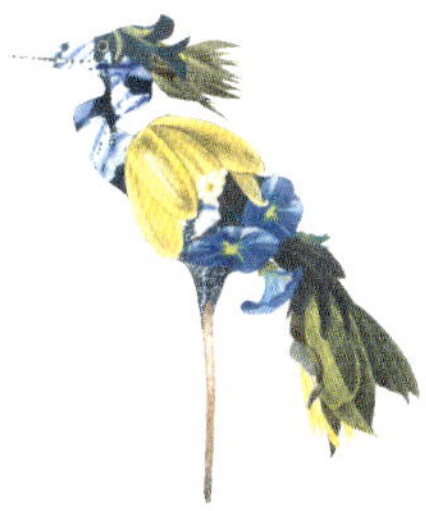

- What is the best thing about God's great gift in Christ?
- How would you tell someone else what Easter means to you?

Live out your hope today.

Let the redeemed of the Lord say so...

PSALM 107:2 ESV

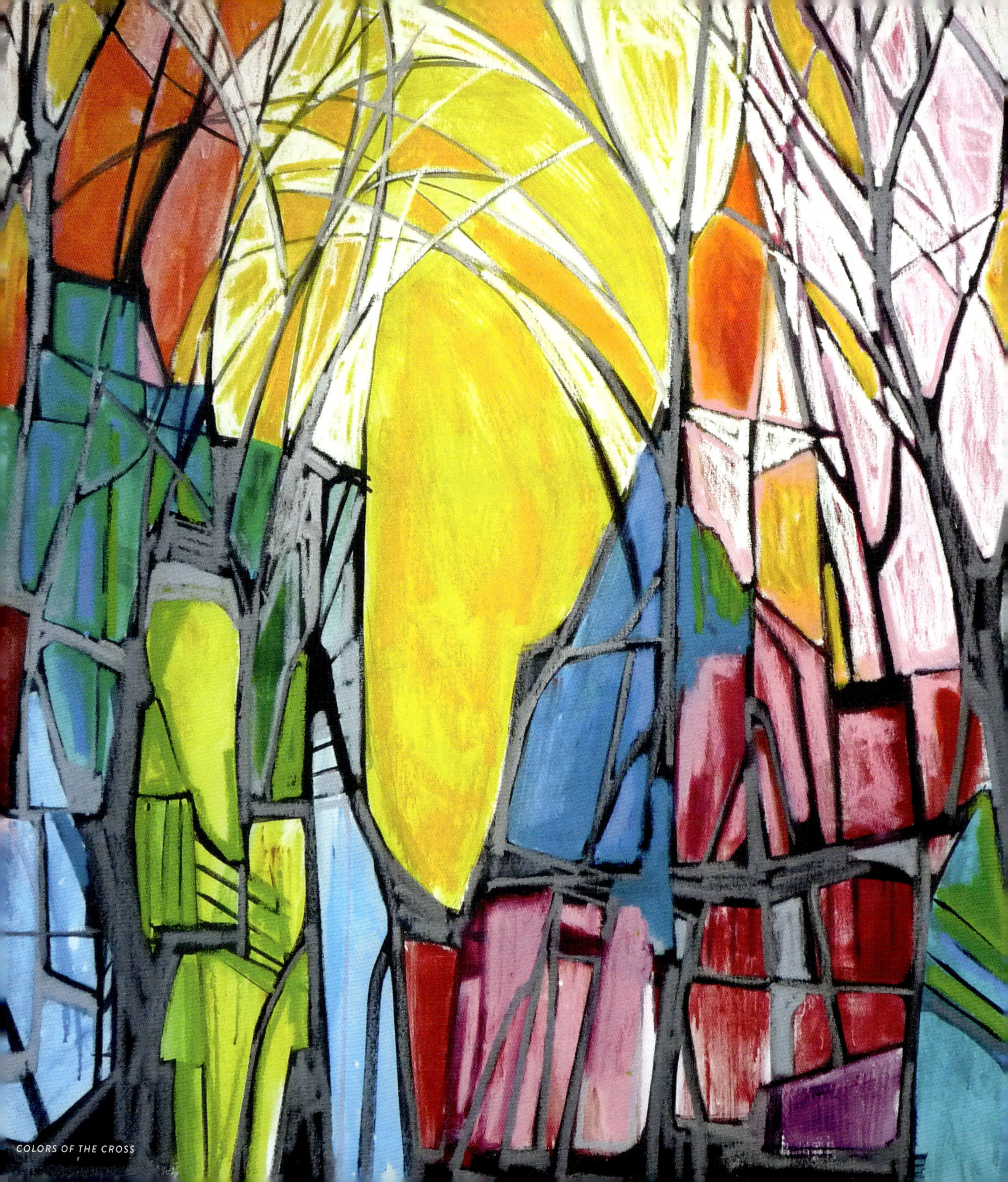

COLORS OF THE CROSS

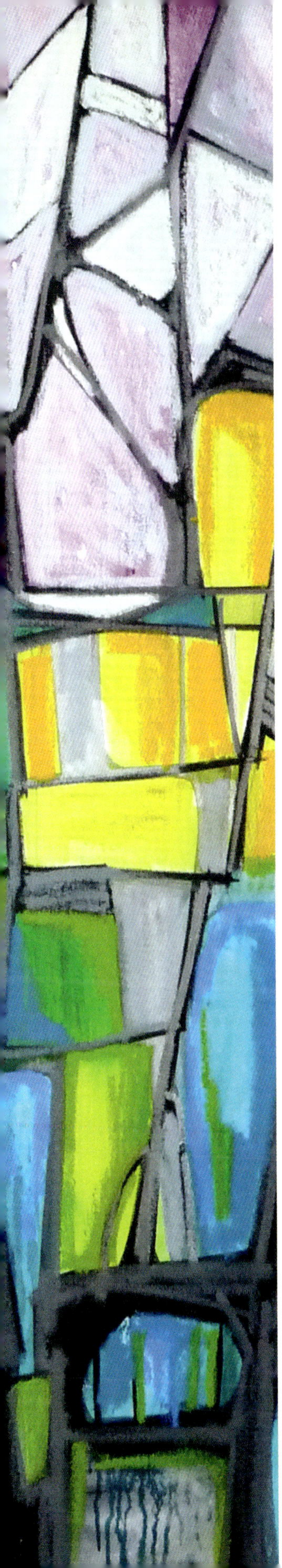

Easter Sunday

COLORS OF THE CROSS

Green palms waving
Grey colt carries
Pink tongues praising
Brown bread broken
Red wine poured
Silver coins betraying
Olive branches witness
White sheep scattered
Ruddy rooster crowing
Dark words mocking
Bronze back offered
Black whips lashing
Russet thorns piercing
Red blood mingled
Purple robe gambled
Sienna sky darkened
Crimson curtain torn
White cloth folded
Redemption
Paid

—Brenda Bogart

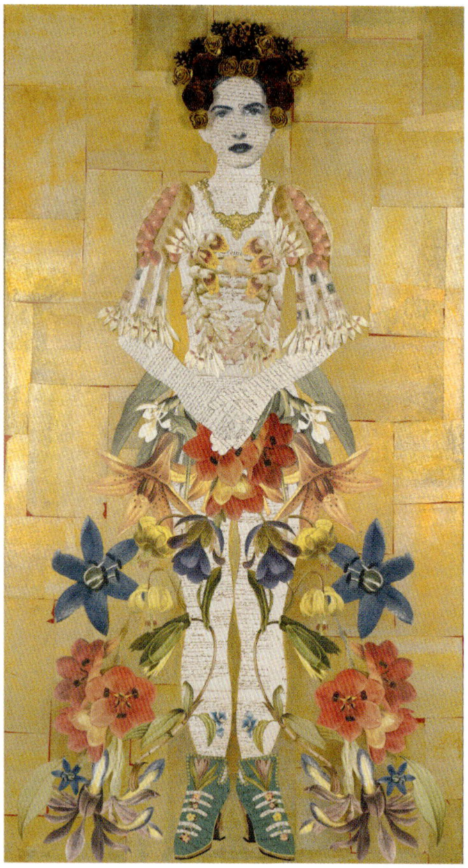

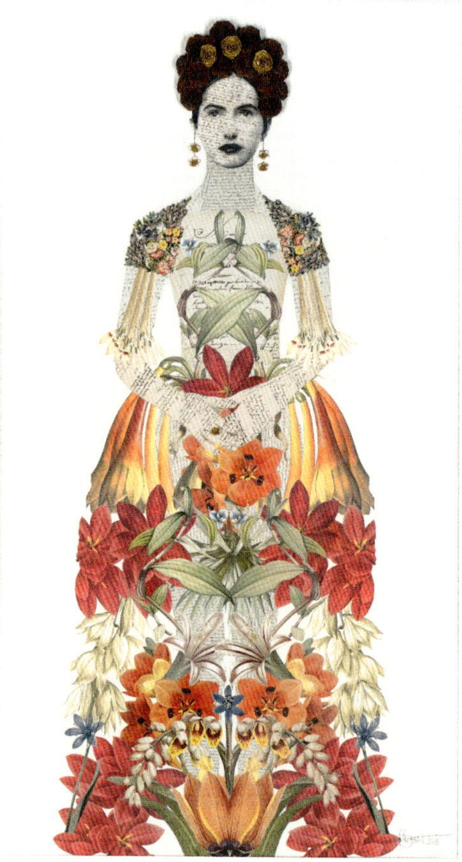

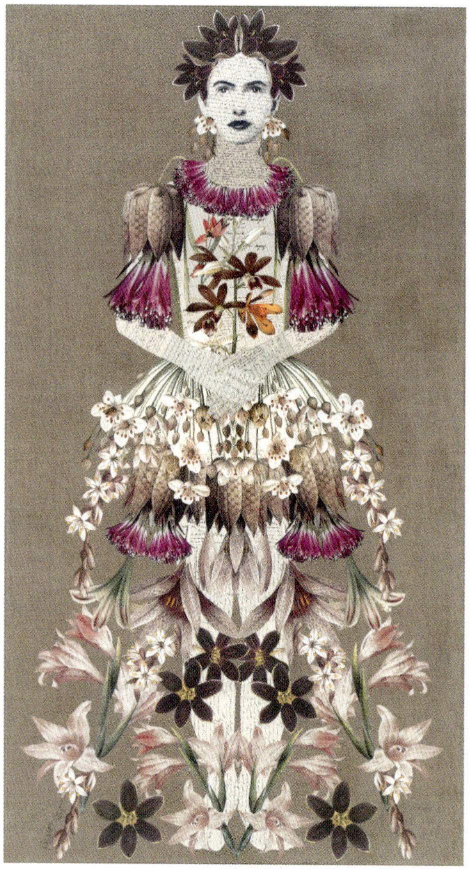

GARDEN QUEENS: *ORCHID, LILY, ASTER*

EPILOGUE

O Israel, hope in the Lord!
For with the Lord there is steadfast love,
and with him is plentiful redemption.

PSALM 130:7 ESV

Thank you, everyone, for following along with me on this Lenten journey! The journey has blessed me more than you know. I pray that you soak in some love this Easter and enjoy your tribe. It's my greatest hope that each of you knows and enjoys God.

I began this project five years ago, posting my art and thoughts with scripture verses on social media. When several people requested a book to capture this journey through Lent on paper, that's what inspired me to create it to share God's truth with others.

My desire is that within these pages you have come to know and deeply comprehend the indescribable gift we have been given through Jesus' death on the cross and his resurrection—not just during Lent but every day of our lives.

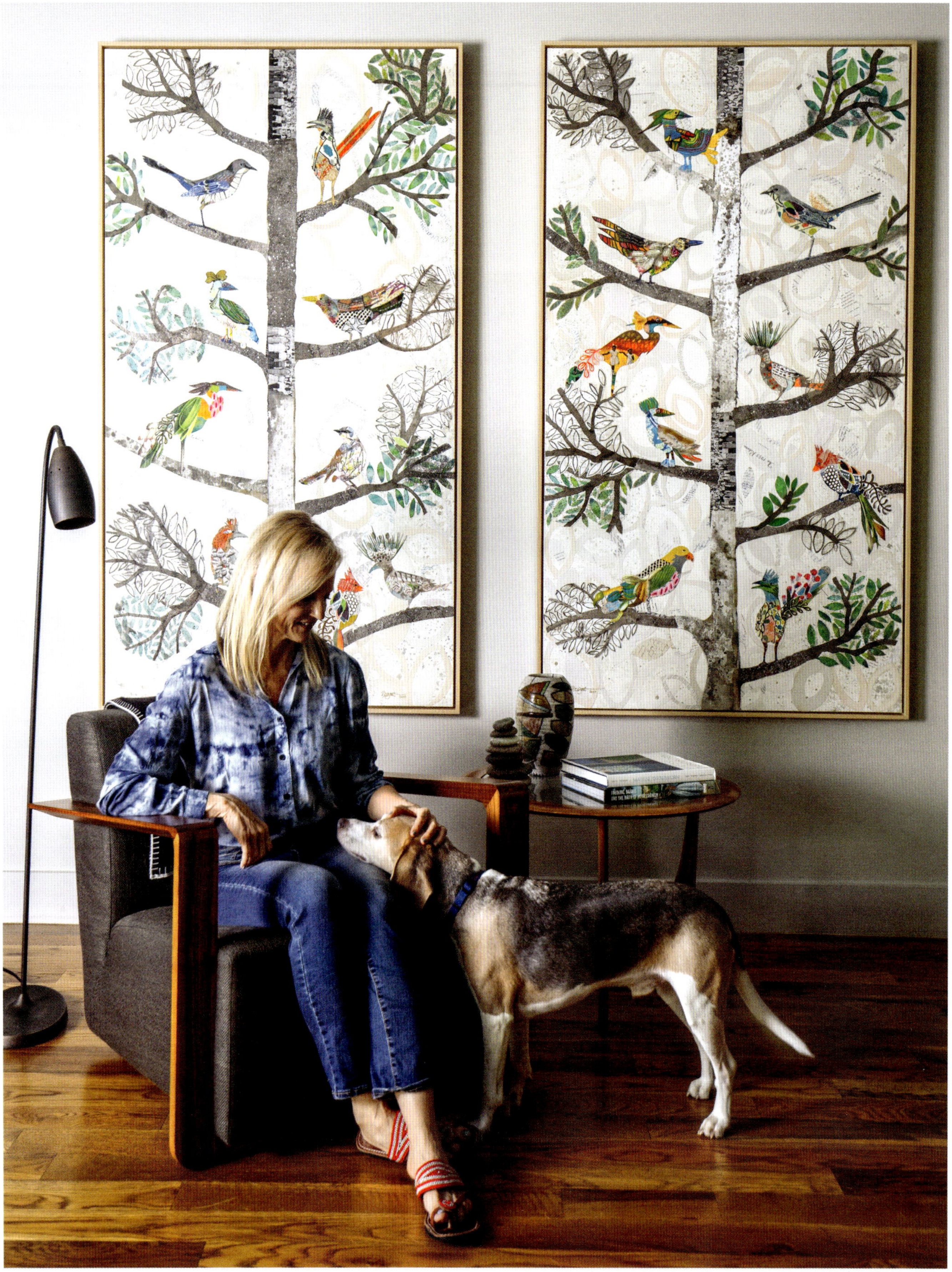

© REBECCA ROBERTS; WITH RANGER, PHOTOGRAPHED IN THE ARTIST'S HOME

ART LIST

For all gallery purchase inquiries, please visit www.BrendaBogart.com.

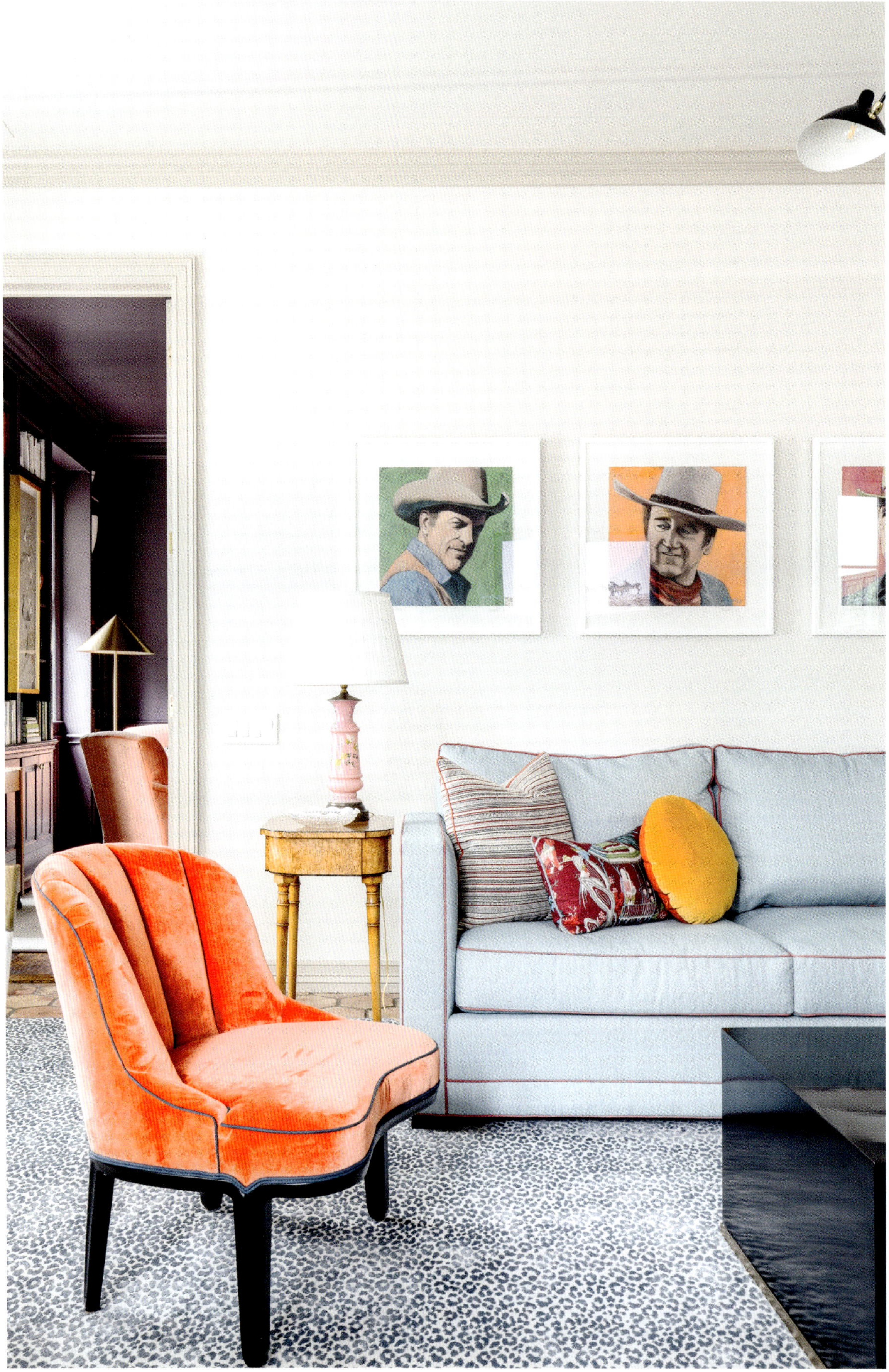

© THE ENGLISH DEN PHOTOGRAPHY (INTERIOR DESIGN BY CHARLOTTE LUCAS; ART THROUGH BLUE PRINT GALLERY)

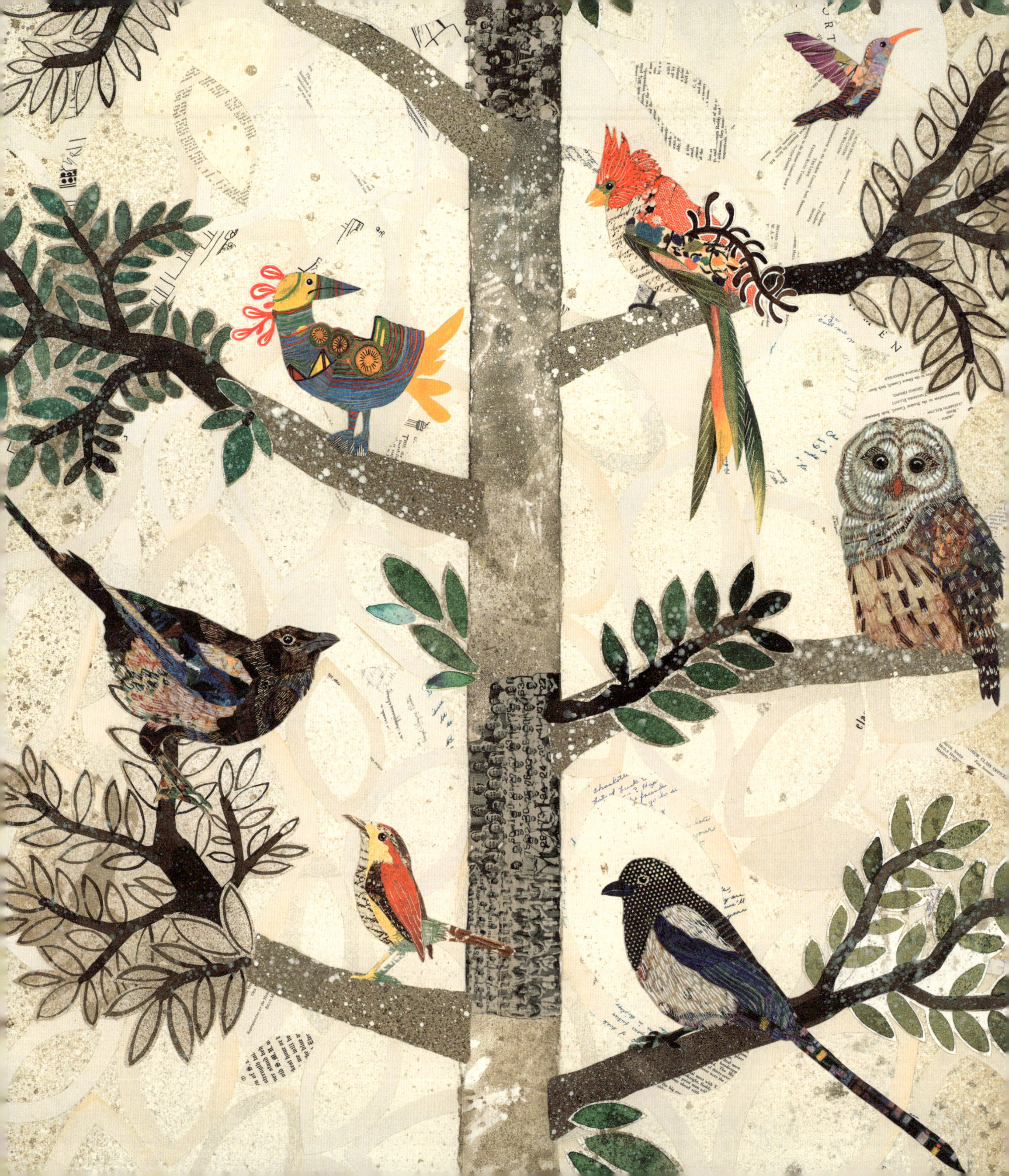